With

compliments

of the

publisher

HARPERONE

An Imprint of HarperCollins*Publishers*

THE
WAY
OUT

HarperOne

An Imprint of HarperCollins*Publishers*

THE
WAY
OUT

A TRUE STORY
OF SURVIVAL IN THE
HEART OF THE ROCKIES

DEVON O'NEIL

THE WAY OUT. Copyright © 2025 by Devon O'Neil. All rights reserved. Printed in the United States of America. No part of this book may be used or reproduced in any manner whatsoever without written permission except in the case of brief quotations embodied in critical articles and reviews. For information, address HarperCollins Publishers, 195 Broadway, New York, NY 10007. In Europe, HarperCollins Publishers, Macken House, 39/40 Mayor Street Upper, Dublin 1, D01 C9W8, Ireland.

HarperCollins books may be purchased for educational, business, or sales promotional use. For information, please email the Special Markets Department at SPsales@harpercollins.com.

harpercollins.com

FIRST EDITION

Designed by Yvonne Chan

Library of Congress Cataloging-in-Publication Data has been applied for.

ISBN 978-0-06-337554-3

$PrintCode

For Lachlan and Dalton.
Live freely and fully, boys.

CONT

ENTS

Brett Beasley cradles his groceries like a baby, strolling the aisles of Walmart in search of the final items on his list. It is January 2, 2017, in Salida, Colorado, a small mountain town on the Arkansas River. Using his hands and forearms he balances two packages of sausage, two loaves of French bread, a stick of butter, and enough boxes of spaghetti to feed seven people. Brett hates shopping and never does it, especially at Walmart, which is why he asked his wife, Cari, to accompany him. She knows he is nervous about cooking for the group, including a pair of dads he doesn't know well. He wants everything to be perfect. So she tolerates his refusal to use a cart or a basket and carries whatever he can't. *Let's get this over with*, she thinks.

The next day Brett and their youngest daughter, fifteen-year-old Brooke, are leaving on a backcountry ski trip with two other Salida families. They will stay two nights at a cabin in the heart of the Sawatch Range, an alpine playground teeming with peaks and powder snow, paying forty dollars a night per bunk. Brett worries, as he does with everyone, whether the dads will like him. But he's also itching to go. The outdoors is his life. He doesn't have a home computer. He's not on social media. "I'd rather be out living," he says.

That mantra has made him a legend in Salida. He's a Harley-riding, Grateful Dead–loving free spirit with a shaved head and long beard who keeps a keg in his garage. A friend describes him as being "everything to everybody," from adventure partner to emotional rock to fun-loving wingman. Which, of course, comes at a price, mainly paid by his family in time spent without him. His absences always saddened Cari, but lately she has felt a shift in her husband. He is more present, more tuned in to their daughters. *He's getting it*, she thinks. What matters most is being with them.

After dinner on this night, Brett, Cari, Brooke, and her older sister, seventeen-year-old Bari, flop down on the living-room couch, nestling into each other like puppies. They turn on a Hallmark movie. It is all Cari ever wanted, this. A life basically too perfect to notice.

──

When Brett wakes up the next morning, it is still dark. He and Brooke finish packing, and Brett walks in to say good-bye to Bari, his adventuress daughter, who follows him up mountains and down rivers like a shadow. She hears her bedroom door creak open and pretends to be asleep.

Ever since she learned of the hut trip, Bari has wished she were going. Brett told her last fall, while driving home from a family wedding, that he yearned to spend more time with her and Brooke. "I really want to develop deeper connections with you guys," he said. He was sad that she was more focused on running cross-country and on her friends than on him. Soon she would graduate and leave for college. He felt her slipping away. "I want to be more a part of your life," he said. "It seems like you're always telling Mom all these things. I want to be that person who you feel comfortable telling." It wasn't the teenage gossip he craved but his daughter's attention and trust.

She heard him. Since then they have become frequent backcountry ski partners, a ritual that both of them adore. Instead of riding lifts to the tops of runs, they climb through the forest and into stunning scenery away from crowds and civilization, then descend through virgin powder snow, as fine as chick feathers. It is the one thing Bari will cancel her social plans for. But she also understands that he doesn't share the same connection with her younger sister, and this hut trip offers him a way in. As much as she wants to go, she isn't invited.

"Hey Bari, I'm leaving," her dad whispers at her door. "I love you."

She lies in bed, contemplating whether to open her eyes and say goodbye. She doesn't open her eyes.

—

Brooke has struggled to be kind to Brett, and vice versa. They often bicker about minutiae. She feels pressured to love the outdoors like the rest of the family; but now, at fifteen, she is establishing her own identity as a musician. Their relationship has shown signs of improving. Last summer they rafted the Green River together, a leisurely float through Utah canyon country, sharing a guitar and sleeping under the Milky Way. When Brett got a toy race-car track for Christmas the previous week, Brooke lay on the floor and played with him. On New Year's Eve, three days before the hut trip, she and her band performed at the Monarch Ski Area lodge, twenty miles from their house. Halfway through the set, as Brooke sang "No Rain" by Blind Melon, her mom, dad, and sister danced before her, smiling and twirling, full of pride. All the trials of adolescence disappeared.

It is around 7:30 a.m. when Brooke and Brett climb into his 4Runner for the hour-long drive to the trailhead. They don't spend much time like this, one-on-one. Brooke is surprised by how good it feels. She has never known how to have deep conversations with her dad. But they're really talking now. He tells her about the skiing he hopes to do around the hut, exploring powder stashes. She sees his excitement. Then he asks her to use his phone and text his boss, saying he won't be at a meeting later this week.

Jerry Garcia, Brett's favorite, croons on the radio. Brett tells her how much he loves Jerry's voice. "He's so passionate about singing."

Brooke has listened to the Grateful Dead with her dad since she was a toddler. But suddenly the music hits her differently. Instead of listening to *him* listen to Jerry, she hears it herself: the full-throated love in each note. It enlightens her, and makes her feel connected to her dad. She asks what he wants to do for his birthday, which is coming up in two days, while they are on their trip.

"I just want to be here," he says, glancing over at her. "I just want to be here, hanging out with you."

PART 1

THE HUT TRIP

A man who dares to waste one hour of time
has not discovered the value of life.

—*Charles Darwin*

1
DEPARTURE

Uncle Bud's Hut, in central Colorado's Sawatch Range, sits nestled in a pine forest at 11,380 feet, eight miles west of Leadville, the highest city in North America. The two-story wood and stone structure is one of fourteen backcountry cabins owned and operated by the 10th Mountain Division Hut Association, a network named for the legendary US Army troops who helped win World War II and trained just north of Leadville. It was built in 1989 in memory of a division lieutenant named Burdell "Bud" Winter, who died in combat in Italy at age twenty. One of the most popular huts in the network, it's a nineteen-hundred-square-foot refuge where families and friends come to escape the rush of society among stunning natural splendor. From the south deck on a clear day, you can marvel at the rounded pyramid of Mount Elbert and the sprawling ridgeline of Mount Massive—the two highest summits in Colorado, at 14,438 and 14,427 feet, respectively.

To access Uncle Bud's in winter, most people park at an old railroad crossing known as Leadville Junction, six miles away, where a snowy lot serves as the Turquoise Lake Trailhead. From there, it's a meandering trek along a snow-covered road to the hut. The route gains sixteen hundred vertical feet and snakes past shuttered summer campgrounds, nineteenth-century silver-mine shafts that are now just divots in the landscape, and crumbling log cabins.

Early on the morning of Tuesday, January 3, 2017, a group of seven—three fathers and four teenagers—met at Leadville Junction before heading up for a two-night stay at Uncle Bud's. The dads were prominent members of the small mountain community of Salida, roughly an hour south and three thousand feet lower. Joel Schaler, a family physician, had delivered more than five hundred babies in town. Chuck McKenna, a former monk, was the principal at Longfellow Elementary, one of the top-rated schools in the state. And Brett, a US Forest Service ranger, oversaw recreational amenities throughout the upper Arkansas River Valley, a sixty-mile-long watershed wedged between jutting peaks. Although Uncle Bud's sat on national forest land, this was Brett's first time visiting the hut.

The trip had been Joel's idea. He and his wife, Laurie Walters, a Chinese medicine doctor and acupuncturist, used to take hut trips all over Colorado. They spent up to a week at a time traversing between backcountry cabins around Aspen, Vail, and Leadville. Then they had kids and stopped going. Seven months before this trip, in June 2016, Laurie had died from uterine cancer at age fifty-nine. Joel, overworked and exhausted, booked the hut to get his family back into nature. He was intent on maintaining the bond with his two kids and restoring a sense of normalcy after putting on a strong face for them. He was also out of shape and decades removed from his career as a professional adventure guide.

Initially it was just going to be them: Joel, his nineteen-year-old daughter, Morgaan, and his fifteen-year-old son, Cole. But as was often the case on their expeditions, Joel invited the McKennas for company. He and Chuck had kids of similar ages (they met in birthing class with their wives) and spent every Christmas together. Chuck, meanwhile, was celebrating his own return to backcountry adventures. Two years earlier, he'd gone in for emergency open-heart surgery, not knowing if he'd come out. A beloved figure in Salida, Chuck had been an old soul since childhood. At age ten, when someone observed that he kept to himself, Chuck replied, "It's better to listen than to talk." The trait made him a trusted ear for many in town who had suffered trauma, including kids who'd lost parents. He looked forward to detaching for a few days, even if he was only a mediocre skier. He was joined by his sixteen-year-old daughter, Melissa.

Like a lot of Salida kids, Melissa started skiing at Monarch Ski Area when she was young. Snow never quite hooked her, however, and eventually she gravitated toward dance and tennis. At times insecure in a community that prioritized outdoor sports, and self-conscious of her ability on skis, Melissa asked for permission to invite her friend Brooke. They'd been close since the fifth grade, and although they spent plenty of time frolicking in the river and hiking the trails above town, Brooke, too, sometimes felt like a black sheep in Salida, because she wasn't as interested in pushing herself outdoors. Brooke was a stronger skier than Melissa, but Melissa never felt judged when they were together. Brooke made her laugh like no one else. They could be silly and carefree, which was what Melissa wanted at the hut. Neither expected her deficient skill to hinder their safety.

Brooke had joined the Schalers and McKennas on a more mellow trip to the Lost Wonder Hut, near Monarch, the previous year—her first time at a backcountry cabin. This trip to Uncle Bud's offered a different allure. For much of the fall semester, she and Joel's son, Cole, had been flirting at school. Both confessed to Melissa, who goes by Mel, that they had a crush on the other. Mel could tell; everyone could. When she invited Brooke, she made sure to add, with raised eyebrows and a knowing smile, "Cole will be there!"

Brooke was attracted to Cole's goofy personality and athleticism, traits that her dad held too. She liked a little of the chase and to make people like her, especially someone as independent as Cole was. She blushed at Mel's invitation; she was in, of course. Cole, in turn, invited his best friend from preschool, Jesse Burns. But Jesse and his dad were going to Belize, so the Uncle Bud's group had room for one more.

It wasn't until a couple of weeks before the hut trip that Brett asked Chuck about joining their group. Chuck checked with Joel, who said sure. *Well, that's a win*, Chuck thought. *We've got Mr. Backcountry himself.*

When Brett told Brooke that he was going, she was taken

aback. She'd been so focused on Cole that the thought of it being a father-daughter trip hadn't crossed her mind. But now it intrigued her: He wanted to spend time with her, on her terms. Maybe this would bring them closer.

Joel had met the Beasleys fifteen years earlier, when they lived across the street from each other. Brett always seemed friendly and upbeat, and he was obviously well known in town. He and Joel waved from their driveways, greeted each other on the sidewalk, and sometimes shared small talk. But they ran in different social circles and were separated by thirteen years in age, so it rarely went deeper than that. Though both were avid whitewater boaters, they never crossed paths on the river. Joel was aware of Brett's work with the Forest Service and reputation as a mountain athlete, however. Morgaan, who knew the Beasleys through their daughters, expected Brett would become something of a co–trip leader, along with her dad, because of his back-country know-how.

Everyone met at the Schalers' house in Salida and caravanned to Leadville Junction. At the trailhead, just after 9 a.m., they divvied up the food to carry in and talked about what meals they were planning to cook at the hut. One of Brett's friends showed up in the parking lot. Daniel Brown was an Alabama transplant who lived a few houses down from the Beasleys and went by D-Bone—or simply Bone. He worked as a hutmaster for 10th Mountain and had to service the hut that day, so he told Brett he would shuttle in some of their supplies by snowmobile to make the trek easier.

The air felt like deep winter—crisp and clear, with puffs

of steam rising from their breaths and the calming scent of wood-burning stoves emanating from nearby cabins. A massive green forest unfolded before them. Other than their voices, the valley was quiet.

Just before they left the parking lot, in case something were to happen, Joel showed Brett where he kept a spare key to his pickup: in a magnetic compartment attached to his trailer hitch. "Do you have one?" Joel asked. Brett's was on a wire under his chassis. Their exchange set a tone of precaution, of being on the same page when it came to safety.

—

Joel, age sixty, had short gray hair, a neatly trimmed goatee, and squinted brown eyes, with a build that still carried a hint of his prime. Before he became a doctor, he spent more than a decade working in the wild. He started as an instructor for Outward Bound, leading twenty-one-day wilderness courses. Then he found river guiding, specifically the world-famous, two-week trip down the Grand Canyon. He ran the Grand sixty-five times, mostly in the 1980s. He'd always been a stickler for safety, and on the hut trip, he made sure to pack extra clothing and survival gear as well as a hefty first-aid kit. When he told Cole at the start of their six-mile approach on skis to stay within shouting distance, part of the reason was because he wanted to be close lest an issue arise that required medical attention.

Joel had been working fifty-hour weeks and skiing less than he would have liked, but he still felt okay as they set out. Morgaan, a petite yet agile athlete, was getting used to her new alpine-touring ski setup, with special bindings that attached only at the toe for the climb, pivoting without friction, before she locked her heels in place for the descent. She had just finished her sophomore fall at Colorado Mesa University, in Grand Junction, and wasn't in great shape. The gear felt heavy. But she was tough like her mom had been, and she and Joel were content to plod along at the back, letting the others lead.

Light flakes glistened in the chilly air. Nobody on the trip was a weather nerd, but Joel had checked the app on his phone's home screen to view the forecast for Leadville, the closest municipality to the hut. It showed a snowstorm moving in the next day, but no cause for concern—three to four inches by Thursday morning, January 5. Just enough to make the skiing good.

Brett and Chuck struck up a conversation at the beginning of the trek. Since their daughters were close friends, they had chatted before, but never in depth. "Thursday's my birthday," Brett said with a smile. His tone was bittersweet, however, and he soon told Chuck why: "I'm afraid to get old. I'm going to start losing things. And I don't know if I'll be able to do what I've done in the past." He was turning forty-seven.

Recently, Brett, who was built like a steel rod, had told friends he felt like he was slowing down. They could see that it bothered him. Though a gifted mountain biker, he never entered local races—the idea of paying to compete on public lands went against everything he believed in. Public lands were for freedom, a sanctuary not to be tainted by stopwatches. Still, he was always at the front of any outdoor adventure, and he took pride in his ability to surprise people with his endurance, whether pedaling, hiking, or skiing. The hut trip presented an opportunity to prove his demise was less imminent than he feared.

Melissa and Brooke, skiing up to Uncle Bud's hut.

On frozen Turquoise Lake Road, Morgaan took a photo of Melissa and Brooke gliding along the groomed track on cross-country skis, timestamped 10:13 a.m. An inch of fresh snow covered the corduroy pattern, barely frosting the pine branches. Cole couldn't resist cruising ahead. He had his mother's wiry build; he packed just 120 pounds on a five-foot-ten frame and had been self-conscious of his boniness in grade school. But he was stronger than his physique suggested and possessed a rare devotion to fitness for a teenager. He'd spent the past six months waking at dawn to do CrossFit and beef himself up for high school soccer. He was also stubborn. In his father's words, "He's not going to back down from a challenge. He's going to keep up with you if it kills him." Of course, that kind of scenario had never actually presented itself.

Intent on looking good in front of Brooke and her dad—and showing his family how fast he'd gotten from working out—Cole took off, then waited until the rest of the group caught up. This was on brand; he had been something of a wild boy growing up. The trait could get someone in trouble in the backcountry, where coordination and communication are paramount. In this case, his father chastised him for breaking from the group, particularly after he had just told him not to do exactly that. But soon enough Cole did it again. Eventually Brett, perhaps driven by ego or insecurity, perhaps figuring someone had to stay with Cole and he was the only one up for it, gave in and chased after him.

From behind on the road, Brooke watched her dad forming a bond with Cole, joking around, the two of them feeding off of each other's energy. It was typical of Brett, who liked to make others like him. He still called most people "dude" (including his daughters), "brother," or "cuz" and thrived on impressing fellow adventurers. Cole made for a rapt pupil. When Brett found out Cole had never been backcountry skiing—the perfect winter outlet for someone so fit and eager—he started to hype him up, telling him how awesome and freeing it was. Cole was struck by Brett's youthfulness. Despite a thirty-two-year age gap, Brett seemed like a kid on his soccer team. They talked about high school and sports and powder skiing. Instead of feeling awkward or pressured to impress his crush's dad, they were bro'ing out. It was the first time Cole had been in a situation where age didn't seem to matter. He felt a weight lift from Brett's acceptance of him. Brooke suspected her dad and Cole would ski all day together.

With a little more than a mile to go, the group encountered a woman skiing in the opposite direction. She was coming down from Uncle Bud's.

"How was the snow?" Joel asked.

"Oh, it was excellent," the woman replied, explaining that she had lapped a gladed bowl behind the hut that led to an easy-to-spot return track for a loop. "You just go up the ridge, ski down, and it drops you into a little valley. Then you swing back around to the cabin."

Her friends had skied a steeper slope into a rugged basin called Porcupine Gulch, she added, but she opted not to join them because of the risk of triggering an avalanche. She didn't mention any landmarks to distinguish between the two runs, nor did the group ask. They had no intention of

venturing far from the hut or skiing anything steep, especially a slope that could slide. Their plan was just to plumb
the mellow, low-hanging fruit around the cabin.

—

It was early afternoon when Brett and Cole reached Uncle
Bud's. D-Bone's snowmobile was parked outside, and he had
a pot of hot water ready for them. Prior groups had shov-
eled snow into piles just off the south-facing deck. Visibility
was limited by clouds hovering above the valley floor. They
dropped their packs and then skied back down the road to
check on the rest of the group, who were still out of sight.

When everyone arrived, the kids explored the hut's interior, with its big windows and various hangout nooks,
claiming beds upstairs. The dads walked over to a large map
on the wall that showed the terrain around the hut. Uphill
and to the north, a long east-west ridgeline separated the
hut from a different drainage. To the east and west, gentle
slopes funneled downhill. D-Bone, who had visited Uncle
Bud's countless times, pointed out on the map various ski
zones and nearby features to orient them.

Hutmasters restock, clean, and troubleshoot problems at
the cabins—as well as maintain the toilet vault, which at
Uncle Bud's was outside, down a wooden walkway, chip-
ping "the cone" of fecal matter that sometimes rises up to the
seat. But they also know the area better than anyone, which
was especially helpful around Uncle Bud's. The cabin is considered one of the easiest destinations in the 10th Mountain

network because of its straightforward approach; however, the reputation can be misleading.

Uncle Bud's sits on a sprawling hillside above eighteen-hundred-acre Turquoise Lake's north shore, about four hundred vertical feet below a treed saddle that divides the hill from Porcupine Gulch to the north. The saddle serves as a critical delineation point, with easier grades leading back toward the hut and a veritable abyss plunging off the other side. A handful of summits and high ridgelines in the vicinity offer visual markers on clear days, but when the sky is shrouded by clouds or snow, navigation becomes substantially more challenging. Much of the terrain on the hillside looks the same—rolling, thickly forested knobs pocked by mini ravines and draws that channel down toward the glacial lake, nearly two thousand feet below the hut. The tall, dense vegetation makes orientation nearly impossible, because you never get a vantage point above the trees, only little clearings that all look the same. It can feel like you're lost in a cornfield, grasping for control that the landscape refuses to give up. Even D-Bone, who knew every ski run near the hut like a mole knows its tunnels, had skied past it unintentionally before, not realizing his mistake until a friend pointed out the cabin behind him, uphill.

After the group settled in, D-Bone left on his snowmobile and headed back to Salida. Three other skiers soon arrived—a couple and a man, all of whom had been to Uncle Bud's before. Together their parties filled ten of the sixteen available bunks.

The other guests kept to themselves as the Salidans broke

into pods. Chuck had just started to write haikus at a table, when Brett plopped down with a beer. He had brought twelve for the two nights; Chuck and Joel, who drank so little that they sometimes split a single beer at a local brewery, brought none, opting for tea. The woodstove crackled. Joel joined them at the table. The kids were talking near the window, out of earshot. Brett saw an opportunity to glean some wisdom from fellow girl dads. He told them he had come specifically to spend time with Brooke in the outdoors. He mainly connected with her over music—Bari was the more athletic one—and he wanted to branch out. Brooke was never very interested in his lessons on how to change a car's oil or fix a flat while mountain biking, and she resisted his attempts to get her to join his adventures.

"How do you relate to your daughters?" Brett asked. "Like, how do you get close to them? I'm looking for insight."

Chuck, who held a master's in counseling psychology, almost had a Dalai Lama vibe. He grinned his easy smile. When his girls were younger, he worked as the school superintendent for a smaller district downriver from Salida, called Cotopaxi. But he was there six nights a week and missed a lot of his daughters' events. So he resigned and took the principal job in Salida. It allowed him more time to spend with Melissa and her older sister, Faith—his priority.

"You hang out with them," Chuck said simply.

"What do you mean?" Brett replied. "What do you do?"

"Shoot, I have dates with 'em," Chuck said. "We go out and get tea or chai, or we go to dinner. I *love* hearing what's going on. I just listen. That's all those kids need; they don't want to know what's going on with you." Brett seemed so interested that Chuck suggested they meet for coffee after the trip.

Across the room, Brooke, Cole, and Melissa were clustered in a corner, sipping hot chocolate on wooden chairs and playing a card game called Rich Man, Poor Man. This was the kind of time Cole had been hoping to get with Brooke. Despite being a year behind her in school (she was a sophomore), they were part of the same friend group and often cruised around town in clusters of ten or more. They rode bikes to grassy Riverside Park and hung out by the rapids, watched Fourth of July fireworks on blankets at the town soccer fields. Neither had dated much, which was why their flirting caught so many eyes. Their friends could tell they'd be *good* together—possibly long term.

Cole's feelings, in particular, marked a shift for him. He'd always been popular with girls—he was funny, genuine, and cute, in a tousled-blond-hair kind of way—but he rarely had time for the game. He would take an entire day to respond to texts, while the girls got back to him in thirty seconds. Most of his crushes never materialized, or they fizzled soon after they sparked. Brooke was different, however. He loved her pretty blue eyes and witty quips. She wasn't afraid to say what was on her mind, which he respected. And her singing voice mesmerized him; he often replayed the songs she posted on social media to hear them again.

He'd considered asking her out on a date, but the hut trip provided an organic first step. Leading up to it, Cole leaned on his lifelong bond with Melissa to bolster his chances. "Put in a good word for me, Mel," he chided. "Like, talk me up!" Getting one-on-one time was unlikely. But that was okay for tonight. Simply being together, in the middle of nowhere, felt special.

Eventually the adults joined the card game, and the room came to life. Giggles and jokes bounced off the walls. Brooke snuck cards back and forth with her dad, who launched into a story about a "secret mission" he'd been given during a fire-fighting detail in Salmon, Idaho: blowing up a horse that had died two miles up a trail with a colleague who kept having to take naps. They had humped in seventy-five pounds of explosives and detonated the carcass into tiny pieces. By the time Brett finished, everyone was doubled over laughing. Brooke nuzzled in next to him, proud to be his daughter.

The interior of Uncle Bud's Hut on the morning of January 4, 2017.

The next morning, fresh snow coated the forest under a foreboding gray sky. The flakes continued falling as kids and dads woke with the light, gradually making their way downstairs around 8:00, nestling into cozy alcoves to relax. Brett liked to teach his girls the essentials, and in the kitchen, he gave Brooke a tutorial on how to toast a bagel on the griddle. "What you're going to do is flip it at this *exact moment*," he implored—just before the crisp took over. He showed her how to apply the butter so that it melted evenly—not too slurpy, not too thin. He was very big on the details.

People sipped tea and read books as others cooked. Melissa felt happiness in the air. Everyone knew this was the day to get outside and enjoy the snow. Brooke could see her dad's intention as soon as he woke up. *Goski. Goingskiing.* He was like a golden retriever that way. She happened to be in the room as Brett changed into his ski clothes, and she marveled at his six-pack abs. *Dang, my dad is so fit.*

Every adventurer harbors a certain impulsiveness—a zest to leave cozy confines for uncertain ones, where danger and ecstasy coexist. Without it, the reasons not to venture out can easily overwhelm the yearn to go. Though Brett's impulsiveness sometimes got him into trouble at home, it also played a key role in his mountain identity. He wasn't afraid to rise before dawn to land a fish or summit a peak at sunrise. And he darn sure wasn't going to miss a moment of powder skiing when conditions lined up as they had at the hut.

The seven of them discussed a plan over pancakes. Normally, any overnight wilderness excursion would involve a trip leader, or TL—someone knowledgeable about the area or mode of travel, with strong organizational skills. Joel often served as the trip leader when he and the McKennas joined forces, drawing on his experience as a guide to deliver safety briefings and ensure everyone was on the same page with their goals and principles. He had been the TL at the Lost Wonder Hut the prior year. For this one, however, no such leader had been established.

Joel proposed a short training session outside before everyone left to ski. They would practice searching with avalanche transceivers—small electronic devices that transmit and receive a signal from other transceivers, or beacons, which were laid out on a table—and "talk about how to be safe in the outdoors," as he put it later. Then they'd head out as a group and stay together as much as possible. They didn't confirm on the map where they would go, but the plan was to meet back at the hut no later than two o'clock for lunch.

Bob Marley's "Is This Love" pulsed in the background. Brett and Brooke sang along as he showed her how his transceiver worked. She had never operated one, and he told her they could practice that afternoon.

Joel had spent plenty of years chasing the spear, courting risk and ambitious objectives both personally and professionally. In his thirties and forties the stress was a good stress: kayaking hairy rivers, guiding groups down the Grand. But after losing Laurie, he wasn't attracted to charging and hadn't tried. His sympathetic nervous system was in overdrive. He just wanted to find calm. He had come to spend time with his kids more than to maximize the skiing, not that his fitness would allow him to attempt anything aggressive anyway—or to keep up with Cole and Brett if they were going hard.

Chuck had a similar ceiling. He had done plenty of backcountry touring when he was a monk—he lived at St. Benedict's Monastery near Aspen, at nine thousand feet elevation—but he'd tried little in the modern sense of skiing powder in wild terrain, which required more knowledge and strength and specialized gear than he'd cared to acquire. Sticking to easy slopes near the hut suited him just fine.

Brooke and Melissa had no interest in skiing at all; they just wanted to play in the snow.

Cole was the only possible partner who could match Brett's energy, having proved as much the day before.

Brett handed Chuck an extra avalanche beacon to use in their drills. It was the size of Chuck's palm, with a few buttons and switches on the front. Chuck had never held one before. Then Brett and Cole, already with their boots on, wandered out onto the deck, where their skis were covered by fresh snow.

Joel finished eating around 10:30 and started to put his gear on. Others were donning boots or waiting outside. He grabbed his climbing skins—long, thin membranes cut to the shape of one's skis with faux animal hair on the bottom to grip the snow and glue on the other side to stick to plastic ski bases—from the drying rack near the woodstove. He attached them to the bottoms of his skis. Then he slipped on his jacket, shouldered his pack, and stepped into the frozen air. He looked for his son.

"Where's Cole?" he asked.

"Oh, he and Brett took off," someone said.

Joel's mind filled with disbelief, then anger. "What?"

2

YOUNG MAN, GONE WEST

Brett had been restless since he was a boy. In nursery school, his teacher described a student who "shows enthusiasm: always" yet "completes work: usually." He spent most of his childhood in Salina, Kansas, a heartland town of fifty thousand near the geographic center of the country, where his imagination wandered. One grade-school writing assignment began, "The coldest place in the world is where I am right now." Other titles included: "My life as an eagle," "My life as a snowman," "My life as a bicycle," and "My life as a baby peanut."

"If the whole world were the same," he wrote in an essay, "it would be very dull."

He excelled at football, baseball, tennis, and basketball and rode dirt bikes and horses. Friends knocked on his door at all hours. "He never said no," says his mother,

Liz. The first time he skied, with two older boys on a trip to Colorado, he skipped the bunny slopes and started on black diamond runs. He cartwheeled down the hill, but kept up.

Brett's father, Bob, worked in manufacturing plants around the country, and much of Brett's view of the adult world—and what he wanted out of it—was shaped by his dad's career. Bob started earning a paycheck when he was eleven, selling Cokes at minor league baseball games in Georgia. By the time he was twenty-two, he was married with three children, clocking sixty-four hours a week as a supervisor for Pillsbury in Hamilton, Ohio—while finishing college at night.

His marriage crumbled under the weight, and he left. He mainly saw his kids on weekends. He and Liz, a plant receptionist, then started a new family. Brett was born in Connecticut, where Bob worked for Nestlé. Two years later they had Brett's sister, Brenda—Brie for short. The family followed Bob's jobs to Minnesota and then, when Brett was nine, Kansas, where the chamber of commerce director met the Beasleys upon their arrival. "Welcome to Salina," he said. "Set your watch back twenty years."

Salina was a blue-collar town, mostly agriculture and factories. The wealthier families, including the Beasleys, lived on a hill though Brett never acted like he was better than his friends who had less money. Bob coached his children's sports teams and still talks about Brett as the star middle-school quarterback. But Bob was away two or three days a week, checking on factories in other states. Brett decided that was too much. "I'm not going to go corporate," he told his mom when he was in high school. "I am going to spend more time with my kids." She thought it was a curious observation for a boy to make.

The Beasleys often camped on placid Wilson Lake, waterskiing and fishing, which served as Brett's introduction to the outdoors. He was tall and tan and cool like the breeze; every girl in town was smitten. "Our neighbors had three daughters and they all had crushes on Brett," Brie recalls. "The mom got mad, because her daughters were fighting over him. It wasn't his fault. He was just trying to live his life on his dirt bike."

In high school, Brett slept in the basement, which became the de facto hangout for all his friends. It had a pool table, couch, TV, waterbed, and resident chinchilla, Ewok. Brett constantly stressed the need for everyone to "chill" but had a hard time chilling himself. He maintained a complicated relationship with authority, especially at home. Bob was a force—physically imposing with a deep, booming voice and dark, bushy eyebrows that tilted down toward his nose. One day, after his parents grounded him for missing curfew, Brett punched the wall in anger. Bob turned, pinned Brett against the site of his punch, and snarled, "I brought you into this world, and I'll take you out of it if you do something like that again." Brett stood down.

On weekends, Brett and his buddies hung out beside a cornfield near an oil derrick, or cruised around town jamming to Led Zeppelin. One Saturday night in December 1986, during Brett's junior year, two of his best friends,

Lance Hassler and Bart Kline, got into Lance's new Datsun 280Z sports car—a two-seater with 170 horsepower. They decided to see how fast it could go.

Bart was popular, disarmingly positive, and naturally athletic. He and Brett played football together and rode horses around the outskirts of town. Bart was also kind. When Brett didn't have winter gloves one day, Bart gave him his.

Lance gunned his 280Z down a rolling country road called State Street, which teed into another blacktop a few miles from Bart's house. He blew through the intersection and slammed into a tree. Bart died on impact. He was 17. Lance, his face bloodied, stumbled to a nearby house for help. Word soon began to spread that he had been drinking before the crash.

Brett, incredulous at the loss of his friend, and his parents drove to the accident scene the next day. They saw where the Datsun had gone airborne after missing the stop sign. They saw the tree it hit, splitting the chassis into three pieces and sending Bart through the windshield. The car was crushed like a soda can, the steering wheel dented from Lance's forehead. Dried blood speckled the earth.

Brett saw in that moment how fast life could change. Just over there, Bart and Lance were in the prime of their youth. A hundred feet later they were flying, at the whim of the landscape, toward tragedy.

Bart's funeral program included a 1934 poem by Kansas native Clare Harner, called "Immortality." Brett hung it on his family's refrigerator, where it stayed for fourteen years.

Do not stand
  By my grave, and weep.
I am not there,
  I do not sleep—
I am the thousand winds that blow
I am the diamond glints in snow
I am the sunlight on ripened grain,
I am the gentle, autumn rain.
As you awake with morning's hush,
I am the swift, up-flinging rush
Of quiet birds in circling flight,
I am the day transcending night.
  Do not stand
  By my grave, and cry—
I am not there,
  I did not die.

The crash, five days before Christmas, was huge news in Salina. Lance, sixteen, was convicted of aggravated vehicular manslaughter and put on probation, but the punishment paled in comparison with his pain as a lone survivor—and the community's judgment.

Brett never stopped hanging out with Lance, as some did. During the year that Lance couldn't drive while on probation, Brett became his chauffeur. He took him to and from school, refusing to make Lance ride the bus.

Brett and Lance went on to attend Kansas State and joined the same fraternity, Sigma Alpha Epsilon, where they lived in neighboring rooms. Lance's roommate was a Wichita kid named Mike Potts, who had attended twelve years of Catholic school and looked like a seventh grader. Potts and Brett quickly grew close. On weekends they canoed down flooded creeks, mountain biked before most people knew what mountain biking was, and rappelled from bridges for fun. They spent their spring breaks following the Grateful Dead in Brett's VW bus or backpacking through redrock canyons out west.

In the fall of 1992, his junior year, Brett met a Tri Delta sorority sister named Cari at a party. She had seen him in a class they shared and, unbeknownst to him, pledged to make him hers. The only hang-up: he had been communing with a different sister the previous summer. Before their first date, Brett got ready in a room with his friend Dave Astroth, who went by Astro. He was nearly yelling. "Man, I got this date with this pretty cool chick, maaaaaaan!" Brett said in an escalating pitch. "I think she's pretty cool, maaaaaaan!" Brett was primping his hair in the mirror, fidgeting with his eyebrows—stuff Astro had never seen him do.

Cari grew up in Kansas City and was studying dietetics, which uses nutrition to treat medical issues. (Brett would major in natural resources management.) She had olive skin, perfectly coiffed, dirty blond hair, and a tender, almost angelic face. She wore Birkenstocks and overalls but no makeup. Cari took some heat from the jilted Tri Delt's friends when she and Brett started dating. She didn't care. She had always committed to what she believed in.

Brett never was the best about calling his parents, but

once he fell in love with Cari, he phoned home. "Mom," he declared, "I've found my soulmate."

—

Days after graduating in the spring of 1994, Brett and Cari packed their van and moved to Colorado. Brett had secured an internship with the Bureau of Land Management in Cañon City, a gritty oil and prison town sixty miles down canyon from Salida. To save money, they lived in a tent with two dogs and an iguana. Cari had arrived with visions of alpine splendor and vibrant downtowns, not the dust and depression she found in Cañon. One weekend in June, she drove to Salida for the annual FIBArk (First in Boating on the Arkansas) whitewater festival, the oldest in the country. It was hardly a cultural revelation—the scene featured a funnel cake stand, music by the river, and a dozen drunk raft guides—but the vibe intrigued her. It felt sleepy, inviting: a funky little sunshine hole in a place known for snow. "We gotta move up the road to Salida," she told Brett when she got home.

Even in a state where every mountain town could be a postcard, Salida's natural setting was unique. The river shimmered in the sun and offered a constant, soothing soundtrack. The piñon forest filled the easy-to-breathe air at seven thousand feet with a sweet, woodsy scent. You didn't behold an alpine landscape just from the hills above town, but from literally everywhere you stood and in every direction you looked. To see it once, as Cari had, was to accept an invitation.

Near the end of the summer, Potts, who'd been crashing at a friend's cabin in Marble, a tiny mining town outside Aspen, called to see where Brett was planning to live after his internship ended. Potts had been looking for rentals in the Roaring Fork Valley. "The cheapest I've found," he said, "is a $1,500 studio in Basalt."

Brett replied, "Well, I found a two-bedroom house in Salida for $300."

"I'll be there tomorrow!" Potts exclaimed.

The two of them and Cari moved in below an elderly lady on First Street, a block from the bars. They were permitted one dog; they had two. They were supposed to be quiet; Brett bought a foosball table.

Brett and Cari outside of their first house in Salida in 1998.

Salida, Colorado, and Salina, Kansas, existed one letter and a world apart. Tucked away a mile off of US 50—"America's Main Street"—Salida was founded in 1880 by the Denver and Rio Grande Western Railroad, which had purchased 160 acres from local ranchers. A thriving downtown sprouted around the tracks, attracting Civil War survivors and European immigrants who sought a simpler life. The Gunnison *Review-Press* soon called Salida "the liveliest town in Colorado." Three hundred people lived there.

Mining remained the area's dominant industry, while farmers and ranchers harvested lettuce and hay and bred cattle. Only after the state paved a road over 11,312-foot Monarch Pass in 1939 did Monarch Ski Area open, offering a rope tow and warming house and the first glimmer of a local recreation industry. In the mid-'40s, the US Army built a winter-warfare training center called Camp Hale just north of Leadville, and many of the base's fourteen thousand troops took the train to drink in Salida's taverns on weekends. (The town also had a red-light district, where local prostitutes known as the Soiled Doves worked until the 1950s.)

Many ranchers hunted and fished, but the snowy peaks and sparkling water remained empty of recreationists for decades. In 1949, a handful of hardy boaters launched the first Royal Gorge race from Salida to Cañon City—a treacherous, fifty-seven-mile run down the Ark that took more than seven hours to finish. Salida was anointed "the birthplace of whitewater sports in the U.S." The best kayakers in the country lived there.

Still, Browns Canyon—the Ark's most beautiful run, with towering rock walls and heaving rapids—was considered too difficult, too technical, for commercial boating. Then in the mid-'70s, a handful of locals acquired army surplus rafts and started to experiment with curious tourists, creating a way to make money from recreation in both summer and winter. But it was hardly sustainable. When the Climax molybdenum mine near Leadville shut down in 1982, hundreds of Salidans lost jobs. Many abandoned all their possessions and left.

The town had no life in it, and tourists didn't want to come to a dying place. The river, despite the upstart commercial rafting scene, remained an afterthought. For decades, locals who lived on its banks had thrown their trash into it. They rolled derelict cars over the edge and tossed refrigerators from their backyards to defend against erosion when the water rose each spring. A three-foot-tall concrete wall in the heart of downtown discouraged swimming—if the exposed rebar underwater from discarded rotten sidewalks wasn't enough.

Salida was stuck in time. To call someone across town, you dialed "9" and then the last four digits of their number. 911 didn't exist. In 1990, a single-family home on the Ark, one block from F Street, the main drag, could be had for $12,000.

Then, almost overnight, word of the cute little idyll spread and prices started jumping up. Locals weren't buying—it was second homeowners or new arrivals who had cashed out elsewhere. For generations, Salida had been known for its churches and bars and a conservative way of life. Suddenly the river and Monarch were feeding free spirits, families. All you needed was a rubber boat and a van, and you could start a company.

"My wife used to heckle me, because I'd say, 'This is heaven on earth,'" says longtime raft guide Bill Block, who started Independent Whitewater, one of Salida's original outfitters, in 1979. "'Fishing, hunting, rafting, skiing. What else could you want?' 'Well,' she'd say, 'I'd like to meet some *people*.'"

It wouldn't be long.

—

The eclectic citizenry who landed in Salida in the early to mid-'90s reflected a changing population across the Arkansas Valley. To borrow a line from the Colorado band Great American Taxi, they were "hippies and rednecks and all kinds of clowns." Everyone had a story: of why they came and, often, how they acquired their nickname. Brett and Cari got jobs at the ski area as soon as they moved to Salida, he as a rental tech, she in the bar. Salida leaned heavily male then as now (women liked to say their odds were good, but the goods were odd), so when Cari showed up to dole out beers and nachos, the local cognoscenti took notice.

One afternoon in early 1995, Cari walked up to an ex–Forest Service worker tending bar in the lodge. Bill Jeffers, better known as Phoenix, ran with a gang of hard-charging bachelors—any of whom would have killed to date Cari. "My boyfriend and I, we're new here," she said. "He loves to do all the things that I hear you guys talk about. Could I introduce him to you?"

Her inquiry plugged Brett in to the cultural core, and Phoenix soon became one of his closest friends. They saw the same magic in Salida. It was cool *because* it was sketchy, not in spite of that. There wasn't a sheen to it like in Aspen or Vail. No one seemed to mind if you stored your old toilet in your yard. It was blue collar like the towns of their youth, except with a skyline to heaven.

Brett and Cari got engaged within a year of moving to Salida, also known as "the Heart of the Rockies"—a moniker that was stamped on businesses, the hospital, even the local snowmobile club. They weren't making any money, but they had everything they needed. Brett captured others' imagination because he sought theirs. "People show their true colors in a blink of an eye. Beas [for Beasley] was just a brother," Kevin "Caveman" Potter, who managed Brett at Monarch, says. "He was straight up. You could trust him with your car keys and your wallet."

Caveman, a six-foot-four, 250-pound welder from New York, looked like a yeti and went on to become one of the valley's top fly-fishing guides. He gained his sobriquet when he told a fellow raft guide that he'd slept in a culvert during a motorcycle trip. "You're just an average caveman," the guide quipped, and the name stuck. Brett mostly called him Cave. "The girls call me Cavey," he explains.

They ice fished after work and became core members of what Brett's friend Mike Reed coined the "recreation generation"—people who had come to Salida specifically for that reason. Caveman devised a career in which he spent 140 days a year on the river, often guiding weekend-warrior clients who created a liability the moment they entered the wild. Some of Brett's contemporaries deemed the stress a reasonable price for getting to spend their days outside on the clock. Brett almost went down the same path. In early 1995, he and Cari decided they should leave Salida. They landed raft-guide jobs in Bend, Oregon, on the Deschutes. When they came home to collect their things, however, something didn't feel right about pulling up stakes. Cari happened to see an entry-level Forest Service job in the newspaper. Brett applied.

Mike Sugaski, a surfer who grew up in Southern California in the '60s, interviewed him for the job. Brett wore a white button-down shirt that looked like it had been crumpled in a ball for a year. He had baby dreadlocks and an effervescent spirit. Sugaski saw a bygone version of himself and hired him. Brett taught Sugaski to fly fish. Over thirteen years as his supervisor, Sugaski came to view Brett as a son, one of the many surrogate roles Brett filled for his friends.

You could say it was unlikely: Brett, the rowdy who liked to party, clocking in for the federal government. But his ethos aligned with the agency's motto, "Caring for the Land and Serving People."

That summer, Cari made $6.50 an hour managing a bakery next to the drive-through liquor store. She sewed her own wedding dress for their ceremony in Moab, Utah. Their families, ten guests in all, gathered at Looking Glass Arch at sunset, just as the moon was rising. Afterward, they ran Cataract Canyon, a forty-six-mile stretch of the Colorado River that cleaves through Canyonlands National Park, with two of Brett's friends.

Back in Salida, they further immersed themselves in mountain life. Eventually the foosball noise became too much, and Brett and Cari were encouraged to find another place to live. They moved into a rented gray mobile home on the river, for which they paid $300 a month. In the evening, they jumped in their canoe and floated to town, shuttling home in Brett's van. They did everything together, at first.

Brett at work for the US Forest Service in 1999.

Brett was a member of the local Militia, a group of Forest Service workers who fight fire when needed, and an alternate with the Pike Hotshots, a specialized unit of frontline badasses who deploy deep in the backcountry to stop big blazes from spreading. During a Hotshots assignment in 1998 he met Chris Naccarato, a fourth-generation Salidan whose family had immigrated from southern Italy in the 1860s. The Naccaratos raised hogs and cattle to feed the miners and railroaders, settling in the northeast quadrant of town, among a population of roughly a hundred other immigrants, which became known as Little Italy. Chris rode a donkey around as a boy, dangling a carrot in front of its snout. Eventually he took a job at the Salida Ranger District, working with Brett. They rallied mountain bikes and dirt bikes or fished every day after work, sharing deep conversations about their marriages, jobs, and, later, kids.

Brett gained a reputation for working like an ox: He was the first to reach the jobsite after a three-mile hike, the first to start digging the hole, the first to tamp dirt back in— even if he was leading the project. He also believed that inanimate objects had feelings, from twisty ties to popsicle sticks, and he grieved for them. For instance, one day while working on a trail, he found himself without any toilet paper. He disappeared for fifteen minutes, then emerged from the trees, bellowing like George Costanza from *Seinfeld*, "I spent a sock!" He openly mourned his discarded cotton tube for the rest of the afternoon. As much as he loved the forest, it wasn't a place to be left alone.

—

Many of Salida's devotees struggled to convey the majesty of mountain life to their families in other parts of the United States. Often they had left a predetermined path that their forebears had followed for generations. Back home, even attending college out of state was deemed a questionable choice. How do you explain, then, what it feels like to look out your window at peaks, beckoning? And at a world-class river twisting through the valley, feeding life and vitality? With neighbors who treat you like brothers and sisters? The adventure offerings were endless and always would be, for the time at hand simply was not enough to explore every alpine lake, run every rapid, climb every peak, or ski every powdery line through the forest. Each excursion delivered a degree of fulfillment that was impossible to comprehend until you experienced it. And then, once you did, it became impossible to let go. Or, maybe, it wouldn't let go of you.

Locals shared a commitment to maximizing their days that was less common on the East or West Coasts, where jobs and careers took precedence. Brett told a friend he wanted to work just fifteen hours a week so he could spend more time in nature. There seemed a fleetingness to life that drove their decisions.

"You only get so many minutes," says Chris Tracy, one of Brett's friends, who grew up in Iowa. "You only get so many sunrises and sunsets. It's a shame to waste any of it."

"We're here for the adventure, not to sit in our cubicle and go home to our row house," says Salida home builder Ed Trail, a Cleveland native. "Yeah, it's a lifestyle, and it appeals to people who like to do stuff. Not everybody likes to do stuff."

Cari had grown up in Johnson County, the nice part of Kansas City, where it was important to buy clothes and look a certain way. In Salida—"a small town with a big heart," as a popular bumper sticker anoints—no one cared. The Western landscape captivated her. She went camping twice as a kid, and never to somewhere like the wide open world here. One of her Kansas friends told her, "When you're done playing Dr. Quinn Medicine Woman, come back to the city." Another was confused. "So, you live *in* a mountain?" "No," Cari explained. "I live in a mountain town."

Cari's parents were workaholics who owned IHOP restaurants before opening a string of import stores across Kansas. When they came to her wedding in Moab, it was the first time her mom got it. "Oh," she said, looking at the grandeur, then at Cari. "This is what you're trying to show me. This is what you want to do." *Yeah!* Cari thought.

Cari took a raft guide's training course on the Dolores River in southwest Colorado but decided she didn't have the moxie to lead others down rapids. From then on, she let Brett guide her—a role he was happy to accept. He treated his interests like crafts to be mastered, fly fishing especially. "Some people just do it because everybody else does it," Caveman says. "Brett got down into the inside of it—different types of equipment, different styles and techniques."

Brett's success seemed almost karmic to his fishing partners, like he put out different energy from everyone else. "I know people who are real frustrated blue-collar guys who don't have a great time out there," his longtime friend Kurt Beddingfield says. "And in the same water, Brett would catch twenty fish." Half of it was belief. He called a plug of rock "Rainbow Island," because he once landed a large rainbow trout nearby. Every time he approached, he'd pump up his boatmates: "This is Rainbow Island, get ready!"

Fishing, however, also wound him up more than other pursuits. He was a knot tier, constantly trying to match his fly to the fish's diet. And he micromanaged his friends. "Farther offshore," he'd command, as they back-rowed frantically to keep the bow off the bank while he cast. "Wag the tail, wag the tail, wag the tail!"

Brett had four dirt bikes, a street motorcycle, three VW buses, a Harley Dyna, two mountain bikes, a basketball hoop, a dartboard with fluorescent lighting, a skate ramp, and a remote-control car track. (Not all at once.) He often achieved Salida's "triple crown," which was to ski, bike, and boat in a single day. Though the town afforded easy access to more than a dozen "14ers"—Colorado's highest (higher than fourteen thousand feet) and most popular peaks—he preferred to bushwhack up lightly trafficked 13ers.

While many of his friends rode plush, full-suspension mountain bikes, he liked his hardtail, and he didn't mind grinding uphill in a furnace—the after-work hours when summer temperatures lingered in the nineties. His friend Dave Carter, a Missouri boy, remembers alpine "fishing" adventures when they'd leave before dawn and hike twenty-one miles and sixteen thousand vertical feet just to cast into shallow beaver ponds holding tiny, easily spooked fish. "I'm like, 'This pond sucks,'" Carter says. "Brett goes, 'I know another one!' Ten miles and eight thousand vert later, I'm like, 'Yeah, it's just like the other one, man. More grass and shit. Got any more?'" They often finished after dark.

In another era, Brett likely would have been an explorer.

Brett managed risk in ways that depended on the activity. His disparate approaches to skiing—where he avoided catching air, cautiously edging over a drop-off instead—and dirt biking—where he had no problem clearing a fifty-foot tabletop at the Big Bend jumps—probably said more about his timidity on snow than his confidence on dirt. There was something of the winter milieu that unnerved him. It would be years before he dipped his ski tips into the area's backcountry scene, which, at the time, consisted of a few diehards lapping the pass.

Salida's recreation generation, like a lot of mountain communities, also saw how their passions could spawn tragedy. Everyone knew danger and traded in near-miss tales, some of which became legend, depending on how ingenious the escape or close the call. But until you lose another human who like you has a pulsing spirit and who does everything you do outdoors, it is hard to comprehend the equation in full—or the actual, devastating cost.

That lesson hit like an asteroid in the spring of 1997. It was early evening on Tuesday, May 13, when twenty-seven-year-old Kurt Glaser ambled down a dirt road to reach the put-in for Pine Creek—the steepest, most violent stretch of whitewater on the Ark. Glaser had grown up in Salida and was teaching his friend Rob Walmer to kayak. Walmer, thirty-two, was an expert mountain biker and the fastest skier at Monarch, where he drove snowcats. In a little more than a season under Glaser's tutelage, he had progressed from running Class I rapids to Class V, the hardest in the area. He was the rec gen's beating heart: He laughed like a jackal—friends could pick up his cackle at a party the moment they arrived—and radiated enthusiasm and kindness, much like Brett, who knew him from working at Monarch.

Glaser and Walmer had kayaked Pine Creek twice the previous week and twice already that week, each time feeling the electric rush course through their veins. But spring runoff was raging, and the frigid water rose daily. At a certain level, roughly 2.0 feet on the yardstick that someone had bolted to Scott's Bridge, the notorious Terminator hole, where the water churns backward like a hamster wheel, becomes a "keeper"—the scariest term in whitewater boating, meaning if you enter the hole, you might not exit. Now it was around 2.2 feet.

Whoa, it came up, Glaser thought as they walked down the trail, staring at the rapid. He noticed one of his lines from two days earlier was closed out—sheer white from the churning boil. "Wooooooooo!" Walmer shouted, giggling, excited to tackle bigger water. The air smelled of piñon pine mixed with mildew from the spray. Glaser recognized the familiar metallic taste in his mouth that came from self-doubt. "Rob should not be here," another friend said as they approached the put-in. Even an extra two-tenths of a foot created a radically different challenge. Glaser knew it would be harder, but he thought Walmer could manage.

The rapid was pushier than during their previous runs. At the bottom of the technical S-turn, Walmer had to make a cut to avoid Terminator. He missed it. The river swallowed him. Recirculating underwater, Walmer ejected from his boat and fought to escape the natural washing machine. Eventually he popped out downstream. When Glaser saw Walmer swimming toward shore with twenty feet to go, having already reached flatter water and appearing strong enough to continue, he shouted, "I'm going after your boat." He paddled for the craft before it floated out of view.

Walmer never made it to shore.

Glaser performed CPR on his best friend that night. Eventually he closed Walmer's eyes. It was the second fatal accident on Pine Creek in two years, with many more close calls.

Walmer had invented a secret handshake that carried on after his death. He called it the Claw, and if you were in the club, you knew: three digits extended, pinky and ring finger curled just so—lock hands like gorillas. Brett was part of the Claw Club. More than an exclusive crew, however, it symbolized an ideal, what they called the Walmer Way. "The Walmer Way was just to get out and do it," says Tyler Lehmann, who'd been close friends with Walmer and later became close with Brett, who recruited him to work for the Forest Service. "Go live. You don't have to make a lot of money, you just have to make enough. You don't have to have the best of anything, you just have to have something to keep going."

—

As the recreation generation stuck their spurs into Salida,

they started grabbing whatever housing stock they could. Brett and Cari bought a two-bedroom, 962-square-foot home on Chilcott, a starter area on the east side of town, for $75,000. When the loan officer asked how they could prove they'd be able to pay the monthly installments, Cari handed over their college degrees: "Well, we have these." It was enough.

Salida still felt more like a neighborhood than a town— now with more than five thousand residents—but suddenly Brett and Cari lived on fraternity row. Caveman was two doors away. Three other Monarch chums lived within shouting distance. Potts and his wife bought a 102-year-old home down the street for $67,000. You could always tell where the party was, because of the thirty bikes parked out front.

Approaching the new millennium, Salida remained undiscovered by the masses. Locals called it Slowlida; Monarch was "our country club," Cari says. Brett tried to recruit friends from back home to join him, touting the town that had changed his life and offering up his garage until they found something else. Mike Reed, a friend from K-State, took him up on it and stayed, but the other Kansas boys declined. It was too far, too different. Too hard to leave what they knew.

Brett's dad, Bob, heard his son's enthusiasm on the phone and often said, "I'm glad you're having a lot of fun." But privately he bristled, feeling like Brett's Colorado life had taken him away. "We thought he was just lost in his own world," Bob says.

Anyone who understood Salida's special sauce saw where

it was headed. How could it not be? The rest of Colorado was exploding. Yet when Salidans told people where they lived, few knew the name. "Where's that in relationship to Denver?" *In the center of the state. On the Arkansas River.* Residents felt like they were hiding out, getting away with a special time. Everyone who had landed in Salida, it seemed, was meant to be there.

One camp held that the boom was imminent: *Any day now.* The other camp scoffed: *I've been hearing that for forty years.* There was a theory, maybe wishful, that Salida was too far from Denver and the Front Range metropolis—the, ahem, five million people who lived within three hours of Salida. Brett always believed each citizen had a right to enjoy the forest, but he wondered, like everyone, what would become of their utopia once the mainstream caught on.

Parenthood was another muddy topic. Any time the question arose, Brett gave the same answer: "I'm just not going to have kids." It wasn't that he didn't want to be a dad; he was afraid he'd love them too much that it would hurt. Putting down his dog wrecked him. What would the vulnerability of fatherhood do? Cari didn't care. She wanted a pair. If she had to parent three to get two, so be it. "We're not going to not have kids because you're afraid you'll love them too much," she told Brett.

Brett expressed his trepidation to friends, who had taken to calling him Freaker Boy when he worked at Monarch, because of his propensity to get worked up so easily. "I don't know how I'm gonna do it," he fretted. "How *do* you?"

Dude, you're gonna be great, they reassured him. *Look at your life up to now. You just* flow. *There's no way you're not gonna be an incredible dad.*

Their first daughter, Bari, was born in 1999 on Jerry Garcia's birthday—August 1. Though thrilled to be a father— "It's the greatest gift that's ever been given to me," he told a friend—Brett grew more anxious and stressed, feeling the weight of also being a provider. Two years later, Cari gave birth to another daughter. Their doctor, Matt Burkley, let Brett deliver her, meaning the first life she touched was her dad's hands. Cari had named Bari after her own dad. Brett named their second Brooke (almost everyone in the Beasley family has a name that starts with a *B*). He loved the word's natural roots—a babbling stream, but also a kind of trout. They called her Brookie.

3
A FAMILY UNMOORED

W hen Joel Schaler and Laurie Walters moved to Salida in November 1999, six years after getting married, it was the first time they had sought to put down roots somewhere. He'd joined a well-known group of local doctors based at the Salida hospital. Laurie, meanwhile, opened a Chinese medicine practice in their home.

Joel, forty-three at the time, had spent most of his life bouncing between rivers and mountains and states and continents. Each time he grew comfortable with a place, his family would move or, later, his work would take him elsewhere—a journey that spanned the East Coast, Africa, Europe, and parts of the desert Southwest. The lack of attachment had a silver lining, however, in that Joel had seen more raw adventure than almost anyone he knew.

His father was a German Jew who was sent to live in the United States at age fifteen to escape Nazi persecution; he later forged a career with the US Agency for International Development (USAID), an arm of the Foreign Service. (Joel's grandfather survived three months in the Buchenwald concentration camp before boarding a ship to the United States that sank in the Atlantic, likely torpedoed by a German U-boat.)

Shortly before Joel entered first grade, his dad took an assignment in Nigeria as a cultural attaché. The family left suburban Virginia for Lagos. Joel and his two older brothers fell in with the local Nigerian kids, who taught them to make slingshots out of tire rubber—and to watch out for cobras and mambas in the jungle where they played.

His parents employed a cook, a housekeeper, and a night watchman. But they also immersed their kids in the natural world. One year Joel's family traveled three thousand miles by station wagon up the west coast of Africa. Later, while living in Turkey, Joel's father rented a fishing boat to explore the Mediterranean coast for a week. They camped on beaches and perused an empty paradise. Joel eventually moved back to Virginia for his adolescence, but when he was sixteen, he and a friend bicycled a thousand miles across France. For five days they detoured to the Alps, above Grenoble, joining a band of young Frenchmen for wine-infused fondue parties and rock-climbing tutorials. They backpacked below jagged peaks, surviving on café au lait and baguettes. Toward the end of the trip, Joel hitchhiked alone to Berlin. He was a stinky teenager traveling in dirty socks, but the journey instilled a sense of freedom he'd never known.

He enrolled at Prescott College in Arizona, one of the

nation's preeminent outdoor-education institutions, and joined its search and rescue team. He learned to raft and kayak, sports that would become lifelong passions. A friend got him a job at Southwest Outward Bound School, kick-starting his guiding career. The summer of his junior year, he led trips into the Appalachian woods for inner-city kids from Philadelphia and Pittsburgh. Joel was twenty; the kids were sixteen to eighteen. Most lived on the street or at juvenile detention centers, with no one to protect them. "My philosophy in life," one of the boys told him, "is you gotta always look out for No. 1." Joel realized then how sheltered his existence had been. It saddened him that a kid could think that way. But it also deepened his commitment: *How do I help him see the beauty of nature?*

—

Joel and Laurie met in the Grand Canyon in 1981, four years after Joel began running the river professionally. He had scored a private permit in the National Park Service's annual lottery, which allowed for a group of up to sixteen. An old friend suggested he invite Laurie. At the time, Joel was a strapping guide in his mid-twenties. Laurie, however, was on a different level. She had grown up in Sunshine Canyon, outside Boulder, Colorado, the oldest of four superathletic siblings. By age twenty-one Laurie was a star on the US Whitewater Team, furiously driven to keep up with the best male kayakers. Her specialty was "wildwater," or downriver racing, and by the time she met Joel, she had run most of the hardest rapids in Colorado, often the only woman in the group.

Joel was taken by her grace and strength as much as her toughness and independence. "She made it look almost effortless," he recalls. Five-foot-six and built like a wire—so thin, in fact, that some people thought she was anorexic growing up—Laurie had a boyfriend at the time, but she and Joel decided to stay in touch. It didn't take long before they became a couple. For most of the next decade, Joel guided in the Grand while she followed the elite competition circuit, racing in North America and Europe. They wrote letters to bridge the gaps.

Safety was always paramount to Joel, who'd had the ethic instilled in him during his time at Outward Bound. His friends came to expect detailed disquisitions before any adventure, where Joel explained their protocols and group expectations.

Joel flipped only three times in sixty-five trips, but all three were in Crystal Rapid, among the most violent in the canyon. One of those flips pinned him underneath his capsized boat with just a small air pocket. The water dragged him over rocks, while he feared any hang-up might trap him with too little air to survive. Just as he began to panic, the river let go and he popped up alongside his boat, gasping for breath. He was saved by an old life jacket that had frayed in the sun, its flotation bursting out of the tattered fabric. He pledged never again to trust his life to worn-out gear.

After thirteen years of guiding, Joel quit the Grand. It wasn't so much the danger—he'd rescued people from flash floods and endured temperatures of 122 degrees, to say nothing of the rapids—it was simply time to move on.

He ran his last commercial trips in 1990. Laurie had earned an undergraduate degree in environmental sciences and then a master's in natural resources economics before changing course. She became interested in Chinese medicine after using it to treat painful menstrual periods. So while Joel was finishing medical school in Denver, she spent three years there studying traditional Chinese medicine and acupuncture.

They reached a crossroads after eleven years of dating: *Either we're going to do this, or we're not*, Joel thought. They committed to each other in 1993, marrying on Bald Mountain near Laurie's hometown. The following year they moved to Grand Junction, Joel to begin his residency and Laurie to start her practice. They also got into backcountry hut trips. Laurie, an expert mountain runner and cyclist, had grown up skiing, but Joel didn't start until he was sixteen—and he didn't start skiing wild snow, away from the confines of resorts, until well into adulthood. Their forays became an annual tradition: trudging into rugged ranges with lightweight gear and hunkering down for a few days in rustic refuges. One year they spent a week traversing between huts with friends. Over time they visited many of the state's most popular cabins, including Uncle Bud's near Leadville.

—

Laurie was forty-four when Cole entered the world on July

19, 2001, four years after his sister Morgaan. Blue-eyed with platinum blond hair like his mother—one of their friends thought Cole was albino at birth—he learned to ski before he entered kindergarten. His parents held him back in second grade, thinking he needed more time to mature intellectually. Laurie wondered if Cole had ADHD, but they settled on "spirited child." He was difficult to corral and a jokester, but not everyone saw humor in his antics. Some of Morgaan's friends locked him in a closet when he refused to rein in his chaos.

Like the Beasleys and a lot of Salida families, Joel and Laurie raised their kids rafting, camping, hiking, and skiing. They took road trips to Yellowstone and Glacier National Parks. Cole excelled at math and science but struggled to express himself. He compensated by cracking wise and disrupting whatever order his teachers or coaches tried to instill—"a little shithead," he once called himself.

Though others tired of him, Laurie, an introvert, took a more tolerant approach. She told patients at her home office that she would interrupt their treatment only if Cole was calling. When he did, she left the room and calmly talked him through whatever challenge was ailing him. Their relationship was far from perfect. But coming from a family that didn't emote much, she always made sure he felt heard, if not wrapped in a warm cocoon.

As Cole grew older, his mischief expanded. He and his friend Jesse Burns established a parkour route downtown. They shimmied up brick buildings and leaped between roofs. They also fired water balloons at pedestrians thirty feet below, snuck out late at night to play "ding dong ditch," and taunted the high schoolers who revved their trucks on F Street.

Sports provided Cole a critical outlet, but the technical aspects also exposed his immaturity. On skis, he eschewed practice regimens in favor of flying. One day he overshot a jump and knocked himself unconscious, erasing half a day's memory. He was twelve.

At Monarch, he trained under Kurt Glaser, who had taught Rob Walmer to kayak and been a star ski racer himself. Glaser tried to get Cole to stop spraying other athletes as he skidded to a rest. Cole never stopped. "Some kids don't have the natural ability," Glaser recalls, "but Cole did. You just had to shape it."

His high-school soccer coach, Ben Oswald, likened him to a badger. When Cole was thirteen, his club team was about to break up, primarily because Cole wreaked so much havoc that the coach ran out of ideas for how to proceed. Oswald, the club director—who had a soft spot for "the ornery ones, who tried to take the piss out of you"—stepped in. "You have a choice," he told Cole. "You have talent, but you're not applying it. I can tell you from personal experience that if you put your troubles into the game, you'll get the results you want." Oswald meant using his frustrations to fuel him, instead of letting them eat him up.

Laurie often shouldered the weight of Cole's misbehavior, but she never tried to change him. She was reserved and asocial in a town brimming with dynamism. So instead of coming down on Cole, she encouraged his independence.

"Trust in yourself," she told him. "Do what you think is right; don't be influenced by other people."

Cole noticed and respected her idiosyncrasies. She always seemed to be in control: of what she ate (GMO free, no processed sugars or meats), what information she allowed into her mind, and what she believed. If she didn't want to ski with anyone else at Monarch—even her own family—she didn't. When she and Joel debated Eastern versus Western medicine over dinner, he backed down before she did. She scrutinized issues of justice and fairness, often vociferously. Otherwise, she was content to let the world spin as she observed. Gradually, Cole adopted those traits as his own.

Laurie also was known as a sort of witch doctor in Salida. People came to her for maladies ranging from poison oak to digestive problems. She handed them a bag of bark and herbs and specific instructions. The brew smelled like old socks and tasted heinous, but it solved their problem with few exceptions.

The family went hiking every Sunday, the same way some families go to church. "One more mile," Joel and Laurie would say, pushing Cole and Morgaan. Joel decided Cole was ready to run the Grand Canyon when he was twelve. With fewer than ten miles left to go in the trip, they approached Rapid 217—relatively tame by Grand standards yet stout enough to produce a five-foot wave that reared up like a cobra. The lip smacked them as they crested it, folding their inflatable kayak backward and tossing them into the river. Joel had hit the wave for a father-son thrill, but the moment he saw Cole in the water, fear shocked him. Worried that his slender son would slip out of his life jacket or be sucked under by a whirlpool, Joel paddled furiously to reach Cole, whose eyes were wide as apples when Joel pulled him aboard.

The trip ended happily, and in the years to come, Joel would reflect on their strengthened bond and shared time in that special place. It was why later they would go on the excursion to Uncle Bud's: to bolster their connection before Cole no longer needed it—or, worse, no longer wanted it.

— ■ —

Laurie initially figured she had pulled a muscle in her back. It was the fall of 2015, and she and Joel were moving a cabinet at home. "I think I strained something," she said. She had been going through menopause and felt depleted. She tried treating the pain with acupuncture, but it didn't go away. Eventually she grew so weak that she could only lie in bed. Laurie dismissed any possibility of a serious problem, citing another woman who had experienced similar issues and recovered. Morgaan, then a freshman in college, begged her mother to seek help—or at least a diagnosis. "What if it's something that will kill you?" she said. "What if you don't make it to my graduation?"

"This is just something my body's going through," she told Morgaan. "I'll be fine."

One night the following spring, Laurie woke up and told Joel, "I can't pee."

Joel drove her to the emergency room. A CAT scan showed

a mass in her pelvis. Further tests revealed widespread tumors in her spine and abdomen. She had Stage 4 cancer.

An oncologist friend of Joel's laid out the options. Even if Laurie could get strong enough to endure chemotherapy, the likelihood of a full recovery and three-year survival was around 20 percent. She'd have to use a catheter until she died. Joel and their children desperately sought hope, but Laurie's wishes were clear. "I don't want this disease to define my life," she said. She only wanted to be comfortable for whatever time she had left.

Joel became her primary caregiver. Cole made her fruit and yogurt smoothies. A friend brought soup. She didn't care much for company; she turned inward, spending most of her final month in silence. One day Cole sat next to her bed and cried, as his parents reminisced about their youth as a couple. It was the lone silver lining to a slow death: getting to replay the special moments together.

Joel and Laurie tried to make sense of why she, one of the healthiest people on earth, had gotten sick. Was it because they built fiberglass kayaks and dipped their hands in epoxy? Because she had kids later in life? There were no answers, only sadness and imminence.

Morgaan completed her spring semester at Colorado Mesa University and tried to decide whether to join friends on a trip to Moab. She knew her mother's end was near, and it frightened her to leave. Laurie told her to go.

"What if you start to spiral?" Morgaan said.

"You can't live in a closet for the rest of your life," her mom said. "You need to keep doing these things."

Cole, finishing eighth grade, never brought up his mother's illness. But one afternoon, after losing a close soccer game, he broke down. Coach Oz hugged him. They lay in the grass, talking through tears. "My mom has cancer," Cole said.

"I know."

Laurie eventually entered hospice care. On the night of June 9, only two months after her diagnosis, Cole's friend Jesse, whom he'd met when they were three years old, came over to spend the night. Joel called Cole out of his bedroom.

"Your mom has passed," he said.

Cole nodded and walked back to his room. Jesse stood up, and the teenage boys embraced for more than five minutes, tears streaming down their cheeks, gripped by emotions they couldn't understand. Neither said a word.

Morgaan was at the McKennas' that night, visiting Chuck's daughter Faith, when her dad called to tell her. Chuck and Faith accompanied her home. Joel and Chuck put a blanket over Laurie. Then Chuck walked into Cole's room and asked if he wanted to talk.

Cole declined. "I just want to go to bed and wake up tomorrow," he said.

For a select group of people in Salida, Laurie's death was the latest in a sequence—a heartbreaking sixth parent from the same friend group to die in twelve years. The causes were random, from cancer to suicide to cardiac arrest. Those who'd been privy to the others couldn't help but wonder whether what some called the town's curse had struck again. The fearful included Morgaan, who had watched her friends lose moms and dads in the prime of their lives. Now it was her. "I had been close to that, I'd known what it was about, but until it actually happened to me I didn't understand," she says. "There's just no way to fathom how that grief and pain feels—the depth of that event."

Joel told his kids, "You're going to have to grow up a little faster now." He took them to family counseling, but after two sessions, Cole refused to continue. "I don't see the point," he said. Joel and Morgaan kept going. Laurie's void served as a brutal reminder of how mothers carry the sky for their families—and triggered plenty of guilt in Joel. Laurie was an adult who knew her body well, but he couldn't shake the feeling that he had failed to recognize her illness and somehow prevent her death. He also wondered whether her resistance to Western medicine had enabled the cancer's progression.

Morgaan tried to talk to her brother. "Are you doing okay? What are you thinking?"

Cole simply replied, "Yeah. I miss her."

It took Cole three weeks to crack the door open with his only friend who could relate. He and Ben Fuller, whose father had died two years earlier in a mountain-biking accident, drove up to Methodist Mountain and talked. "I know there's nothing I can say to help it," Fuller told him. "But just know that your mom would want you to be happy."

The only place where Cole felt like himself was on the soccer field. He made varsity as a high school freshman and stretched the field with his speed.

Aside from Cole's friends, the most likely conduit to his

feelings was Chuck. He tried time and again to reach Cole, as he'd done with other bereaved kids. "How ya doing?" he asked gently, when he saw him at his house or in a private moment.

"I'm doing fine. It's okay," Cole responded, before moving on to something lighter.

Chuck knew enough not to prod; deflection is a psychological defense mechanism that Chuck had used himself after his ten-year-old brother died from cancer when Chuck was sixteen. He didn't process that death until he was in his thirties.

"Okay," Chuck told him. "But I've worked with a lot of people, Cole, and you can't go around this. At some point, you're going to have to go through it."

4

GIRL DAD

There is a psychological term for men like Brett. It's called *puer aeternus*, and it translates from the Latin to "eternal child." The Swiss psychoanalyst Carl Jung used it in 1951 to describe people who seek freedom and independence—and sometimes can't live without it. They tend to be attractive and charming and have a hard time making decisions. Salida is full of puer aeternuses. What's harder to define is the cost of being one.

Marie-Louise von Franz, a colleague and disciple of Jung's, wrote a book in 1970 called *The Problem of the Puer Aeternus*. She argued, as Jung had, that the refusal of puers to grow up stunts their growth as adults and leads them to avoid meeting problems head-on.

Brett struggled with Bari's and Brooke's younger stages, feeling like his daughters slowed him down, even as he adored them.

"Why don't they want to go dirt biking?" he wondered to Cari.

"Because you don't take them dirt biking."

"Well, it's scary," he said. The girls were four and six.

"Yeah, that would be scary," she replied.

Brett, Cari, Bari, and Brooke pose for the
Beasley family Christmas card in 2008.

Bari and Brooke called themselves "dirt children" as they grew older. Their home backed to a lumberyard, where they found trash and built "cat hotels" for the feral felines prowling the area. During multiday raft trips they slathered themselves in mud and ran around, their joyful shrieks echoing off the canyon walls. Brett nicknamed Bari "Shmari," which morphed into "Shmara" or "Shmare." "Brookie," meanwhile, became "Cookie" then "Klukie" and, finally, "Kluke Monster." They adopted their nicknames as a symbol of their dad's affection. When Cari was working as a nurse in Leadville or otherwise out of town, Brett and his girls lounged on the couch and watched *Cops* or NASCAR, dipping Doritos in ketchup. At night, they lay down in Bari's room, and Brett strummed Grateful Dead lullabies until his babies fell asleep.

As a boy in Kansas, Brett had been spanked and bitten by his mom (to show how much the latter hurt when he did it to his sister), picked up by his ears by a teacher, and forced to wash out his mouth with soap when he swore. But none of that robbed him of his softer side. When his girls misbehaved, he simply said, "That makes me sad," and then let it sink in for them.

On the surface, Brett had a beautiful family, his dream job, and a galaxy of friends—in a perfect little town that reminded everyone of Mayberry. But he struggled to keep up. One of Brett's biggest issues was overscheduling himself to the point of angst. He kept his cell phone at night in a room downstairs from their bedroom, and each morning, around six o'clock, Cari would hear it start to ding—usually with invitations to ski or ride or fish. His inability to say no became a daily prison. Not only did he hate missing an adventure, but he also feared not being included next time. Once, when two friends of Bari's stopped by to borrow his skateboards but didn't ask him to join them, he was so sad that Bari had to console him.

Fourth of July was always a hard holiday, because Brett insisted on attending every party that he was invited to—a classic sign of a puer. "He liked everyone loving him," Cari says. "And he didn't want to disappoint anyone by not showing up."

Later, all the *up, up, up* had to come down. Brett tended to replay every social interaction he'd had. "How do you think I was perceived?" he asked Cari. "What do you think this person meant when they said that? Should I have said what I said? Do you think I hurt their feelings?" Cari talked through it until she could no longer. "I have listened to you and I can't keep doing this," she told him.

Mainly, Brett just loved pleasing people.

Part of his appeal was being unpredictable. He showed up for mountain bike rides bare chested, wearing cotton shorts and sipping from a coffee mug in his bottle cage—no water. His helmet had lost its plastic cover, leaving just white Styrofoam. He looked like a kook, but Brett called it "going Lynyrd Skynyrd," which was not to be confused with "going NASCAR," an ode to his habit of walking around shirtless, showing off his ink. He had a full tattoo sleeve on his right arm and a partial sleeve on his left, as well as biker flames, a pair of beetles for the girls, and homages to the Grateful Dead on his back. Combined with his shaved head and long beard, the tats presented the tough exterior he wanted—especially when he rode his Harley. "Do I look scary?" he asked Cari, hoping for confirmation.

He played guitar in the Presbyterian church band, and hosted garage jam sessions at least twice a week. A favorite song to pick was "Dark Hollow," by the Dead, which eschewed city life and tight confines.

Some of Brett's contemporaries vanished from their social scenes because of the unrelenting onslaught of parenthood. "There were times when I just said, 'Don't call me again' to my friends," Caveman recalls. "It was tough, but in life you gotta make your choices. You can't keep 'em all happy. And you don't wanna make Mama mad." Brett, on the other hand, kept so many friends happy that it frustrated those he felt closest to. "He was a social butterfly," Mike Potts says. "Sometimes it was good. Sometimes I was bummed because he didn't have time to make it to something I wanted to do."

Even in a town that prized full days, no one filled every increment of every day like Brett. He wasn't content to simply accept what life allowed him if there was more to experience. People admired him for a lot of reasons, but perhaps none more so than that—even when it created imbalance.

Brett often went fishing after work with Naccarato, a trusted confidant, and lamented that he wasn't connecting with his girls. Friends encouraged him to skip a night of play, stay home with his family. But he couldn't help himself. His fear of missing out was overwhelming. "I'm like, 'Well, I'm gonna be fishing. Kurt's going fishing. We got a bunch of beer,'" Naccarato remembers. "He'd literally be like, 'Fuck, fuck. All right, I'll talk to Cari. I'll talk to Cari.' And then he'd show up. He'd come running in, we're getting ready to put on, he's got his rod, just kinda Brett chaos, throwing shit in the boat, frantic, like, 'We gotta go! Let's go fishing now!'" While Cari supported who he was and never spoke poorly of him, her friends quietly wondered how long she could take it.

Brett's whims could be altruistic, too. He heard about a buddy building a deck and stopped by to pound nails for five hours. Or he mowed his neighbor's lawn. When Naccarato asked for help chucking concrete from a busted-up sidewalk into a utility trailer, "Maybe the other four people I called wouldn't show up, but Brett was there," he says. "You *knew* you could count on him."

"We always talked about Brett being Salida's unofficial mayor," Ben Lara, his supervisor at the Forest Service, says. "Anytime you'd go out for a drink, you didn't really talk to him, because he was talking to everybody else."

In a strange way, Cari and their girls suspected that Brett's spending time away from his family was a protective shield. "It was almost like he loved us so much that it gave him anxiety, so it was easier for him to be less present," Brooke says.

—

As with most teenagers, Bari and Brooke butted heads with their dad, often over little things. He constantly bickered with Brooke about cleaning her room. One night, Bari refused to eat a chili he'd made because it contained too many stewed tomatoes. He didn't let her go out until she ate his chili. Another time, he wanted to hang out with her but she wanted to meet a friend and asked him for a ride. He was hurt. Instead of saying that, however, he confiscated her running shoes.

He always seemed to be rushing around, but he also showed the girls the value of slowing down. He let strangers cut in front of him in the lift line at Monarch—an unheard-of move by a local—and he drove like an elderly person, hesitant, at a crawl. Cari had encouraged Brett for years to temper his expectations. "Not everything is what you want to do, going a hundred miles an hour," she told him. "Sometimes it's a small adventure, but you're with your girls." That finally resonated on the river. Brett taught Bari how to row when she was thirteen—as well as how to read water and when to use the current and eddies. They floated from Big Bend to town two miles away in the family raft, *Peely Dan*, so named for its constantly detaching rubber. Then they lifted the boat over their heads and carried it home.

Brooke, meanwhile, assumed her dad's affability. "She was just this uber confident child," Cari recalls. "People would gather around her and she would tell them how it was."

Brett wore his Dad Goggles proudly. His girls were brave enough to hitchhike (which he did with them multiple times when his bus or bike broke down), *and* they were brilliant. On their way out of their favorite breakfast haunt, Patio Pancake, Brett couldn't help but stop at every table. "Yeah, she has straight A's," he gushed, as Brooke whispered, "Please, can we go?" He wasn't trying to make anyone jealous. He just liked showing her off.

Even on nights when he stayed in his garage, jamming into the wee hours with friends, he still slipped into his daughters' rooms and kissed them goodnight.

"I'm sleeping," Brooke groaned. "It's 3 a.m.!"

"Sorry," Brett whispered. "I have to say I love you."

—

Brett's job was demanding—he managed recreation across the district, from campgrounds to outfitters to high-alpine trails. "I felt as if he was a surgeon on call," Cari says. "I was like, dude, you don't have to work this much." His former district ranger, Jim Pitts, says Brett "literally did the job of two people 100 percent of the time."

He oversaw dozens of full-time and seasonal employees, designed and built some of the area's most popular trails (periodically with the help of prison labor), and served as the agency's face in the community. One day while driving up Poncha Pass, he showed Tyler Lehmann, then a first-year off-highway-vehicle (OHV) crew member, how he did it. He put on his Forest Service uniform over a shirt from the band Tool. Lehmann happened to be wearing a Metallica shirt. "On the inside," Brett said, "you let your mind do what it has to do, and you go to your place. But you've got this uniform on the outside." He donned his hard hat, tilting it ever so slightly to the side, another stake of independence. He never neglected his duty, however. Before giving a speech, lest the crowd draw any preconceived notions from his shaved head and tattoos, he slipped on a pair of eyeglasses to look smarter.

Many of his colleagues struggled to bridge gaps between dueling land users. But he could relate to them all, so instead of viewing him warily, they let him in. This was especially true in the motorized community, which often felt it was fighting an uphill battle for trail access: Brett was an expert with street cred.

"He used to describe the environmental group as the whale painters of the world," Lara says, referring to ardent conservationists. "But he valued that perspective and what they fought for, and he would call those people his brothers. He would also look at users with opposite views, and call them his brothers too. It's a lot to handle in one person's head—to appreciate all sides of something. And it was genuine."

Generally, the professional arc of a Forest Service lifer, which Brett became over time, darts around the country. To remain in one district for more than a decade is rare. Many of Brett's colleagues suspected he could someday run the district, but he didn't want to be a politician. One of his early bosses pulled him aside and said, "You and I, we don't belong in the office. We're diggers." Brett loved that word. He was perfectly content being a GS-9 on the federal pay scale, earning around $60,000 a year, far below the GS-13s and -14s—or, as he called them, "GS-Fantastics"—who made six figures.

He did once consider leaving the agency to become a teacher. But his love of the land wouldn't let him. For the same reason he preferred not to travel—"Why would I go somewhere else when I have everything right here?"—he prioritized place over career. Salida still felt like Valhalla.

—

Brett's initial inkling that he might be slowing down physically came in his side gig. For almost a decade he had battled big blazes around the West, sleeping on the ground in sweat and dirt for weeks at a time. The money was great, his expenses were nil, and Cari held down the homestead. Then one day he came home from a fire in Idaho and said he wasn't sure if he could do it anymore—wake up at 5 a.m. and dig trenches all day on the front lines. He was in his mid-forties. "It was the first time I'd heard him be, like, 'I'm getting too old. This is hurting me,'" Cari says.

Brett told friends he was having a tougher time recovering. He complained about upstarts two decades younger surpassing him. Perhaps the only activity in which he still felt as capable was backcountry skiing. Brett had grown bored with resort skiing—standing in line to ride lifts and ski the same runs over and over, often on hardpacked snow that made joints ache. Backcountry skiing was none of that. It took place in empty, snow-plastered forests and along high-alpine ridgelines with your best buddies, usually under bluebird skies. Brett had to sweat for his turns and know where the powder lingered after a storm—challenges he rel-

ished. The physical reward comes close to levitation: float-
ing through weightless, virgin snow, down a mountain that
feels like your own.

Backcountry ski pioneer Dolores LaChapelle, who lived
in Colorado, likened it to what a bird must feel flying across
a mountain. "Powder snow skiing is not *fun*. It's life, fully
lived, life lived in a *blaze of reality*," she wrote in her semi-
nal 1993 book *Deep Powder Snow*. "What we experience in
powder is the original human self, which lies deeply inside
each of us, still undamaged in spite of what our present cul-
ture tries to do to us. Once experienced, this kind of living
is recognized as the only way to live—fully aware of the
earth and the sky and the gods and you, the mortal, playing
among them."

Bari was a junior in high school when Brett started inviting her to go backcountry skiing with him. He realized he
had given away days he could have spent with his daughters
and couldn't get back. But he would try. They parked on
Monarch Pass and climbed to the Crest, continuing north
to an area called Perfect Trees, where the Forest Service had
thinned the vegetation and created ten-foot-wide hallways
between evergreen stands that ran from top to bottom and
looked like they had been combed. For so long he'd pushed
Bari beyond where she wanted to stop, knowing that she
was capable of more. Suddenly they merged. She could keep
up. Tours with her satiated him, not just fatherly but physically. He flashed his trademark shaka signs, hang loose, at
the top and snapped selfies of the two of them. Cari saw a
broader shift. "It was the joy in his face," she says, "like,

This is it! I finally have my buddy who I can do stuff with all the time."

They started going out almost every weekend.

Brett was an old-school telemark skier (meaning his heels were free), and he dressed like it. He owned multiple pairs of leather two-buckle boots, which, functionally speaking, had been outdated for twenty years, replaced by burlier plastic. He skied in a light, raggedy jacket. His pants were covered in duct tape. It was an expression as much as a mindset, and everyone loved him for it.

His friends who had been backcountry skiing for longer sought out steeper lines, but Brett never wanted to tussle with avalanches, or even the chance of them. Colorado has the deadliest snowpack in the country because of how dry the snow is, and he feared it. The same lack of moisture that creates euphoric skiing prevents overlapping layers of snow from bonding to each other. This makes slabs more prone to gravity's omnipresent tug, especially on slopes over thirty degrees and when a human trigger is present. Nearly twice as many people have died in avalanches in Colorado than in any other state, an average of six per year. Backcountry skiers and snowboarders are the most often killed. Experts will tell you it doesn't matter how much someone knows about snow; the best they can do is guess whether it's stable or not.

Sometimes Brett bumped into his buddy Mike Reed on the pass, both skiing alone. Reed had developed a deep understanding of the snowpack years earlier. "How do you know it's safe?" Brett asked.

"You would think he knew," Reed says, "but backcountry skiing wasn't in his wheelhouse yet." Lehmann adds, "It may have been the only sport he tried that he wasn't the best at."

Brooke, meanwhile, never got sucked in the way Bari did. But as she watched her sister and father grow closer through backcountry skiing, a seed of jealousy formed. She wanted to feel that connection too. She and her dad played disc golf at the Salida course, and they always had music and the river. In the summer of 2016, before Brooke's sophomore year, the two of them joined Mike Potts, Kurt Glaser, and a host of other families for a float down Desolation Gray Canyons, or Deso-Gray, in Utah. The trip coincided with the Rio Olympics, and during a layover day, they staged their own games, highlighted by the long jump. Most adults took one listless hop and called it a contest, but Brett ended up in a marathon duel with a sixteen-year-old competitive swimmer. He stretched between jumps and counted off his steps to takeoff, as the crowd wheezed from laughter. The boy prevailed, barely, to raucous cheers; but Brett redeemed himself in the rock shot put and beer-can-crushing competitions.

Brett also brought his guitar on the trip, and Glaser tried to get him to play at night. He didn't like singing in public, so he refused, instead persuading Brooke to play. Everyone gathered around the fire as she strummed and crooned. Her dad watched quietly from the side, glowing with pride.

When Brett joined the hut trip a few months later, both he and Brooke hoped for more memories like those.

PART 2
THE SEARCH

Nature is reckless of the individual. When she
has points to carry, she carries them.

—Ralph Waldo Emerson

5

TRAPPED

*T*he decision didn't require much debate. It's a rare morning to wake up with fresh snow at a backcountry hut and
nothing to do but ski. The whole point of the trip was for
dads to be with their kids, but that was overridden by powder
fever. Brett and Cole had known each other for barely twenty-
four hours, yet they fed off each other's verve. Standing on the
deck after breakfast, looking out at the Sawatch Range under
milky skies, both felt giddy with excitement. Brett, the pleaser,
who wanted people to see him as cool, flashed a grin. "You
wanna ski a lap?" For a moment, Cole hesitated. Should I wait
twenty minutes for everyone to finish gearing up? he wondered.
But he couldn't resist. "Yeah," he replied.

They headed north from the hut, up a gentle, forested, four-
hundred-foot rise. Snow began to fall more steadily as they
climbed. They pointed to their left with their poles at the mellow pitch they intended to ski, agreeing that it looked safe and

straightforward. They would start from the broad, rounded saddle that separates Uncle Bud's from Porcupine Gulch and ski south, away from the much steeper drop down the north side into Porcupine.

Porcupine Gulch is shaped like a giant U, with an open eastern end and steep ridgelines rising on the south and north sides. A rocky headwall beneath 12,893-foot Galena Peak closes off the western corner—the bottom of the U, as it were. Porcupine's belly looks like a bathtub and is cleaved by meandering Porcupine Creek, which starts under Galena and runs east. The entire drainage is about one mile wide, three miles long, and a thousand feet deep, with hundreds of acres of spooky, mossy, boulder-filled forest on its floor. In the summer, it's a place to escape civilization, hike off trail, and camp in grassy meadows among elk, moose, and bears, miles from the closest human. But that same solitude and rugged topography make it a ruthless place to be in winter.

Cole had never done a real backcountry ski run. Unlike the day before, when he'd taken the lead on the groomed road to the hut, now he was following Brett, the spirited Jedi, into a wild area, where they would ski some of the deepest powder of his life.

As they neared the saddle, they curled left into thicker trees to get out of the wind, stopping in a small clearing where they could remove their skins to begin their descent. The tall conifers prevented them from seeing the low-angle run they intended to ski. It also placed them on a flatter plateau, without clear north and south declivities like the saddle featured elsewhere—a recipe for disorientation. Brett tried to teach Cole how to peel his skins off his ski bottoms while keeping his skis on. Like an instructor, *he balanced on one leg while lifting the other leg high enough to grab the skin and rip, explaining the technique as he went. Cole appreciated the lesson but failed to master the awkward motion. No matter. They transitioned in haste; both were itching to descend, to feel the thrill of bottomless snow.*

Brett pushed off and then Cole followed, slowly picking up speed as the gentle pitch increased. Cole left Brett's track to plumb untouched powder. The rush was unlike anything he had experienced—it filled his whole body. He and Brett hooted with joy as they snaked down the mountain in tandem, spraying rooster tails at the apex of each turn. This was why they'd slipped away. To feel suspended above the earth but below the sky.

Their bliss lasted for about a minute, and then Brett began to cut left, wanting to ensure he intersected the track that would lead them back to the hut. Cole trailed behind him.

Brett could feel them trending lower, away from their perceived target. He stopped and pictured the loop, which was already taking much longer than he expected. "Theoretically, we're here," he said, imagining them near the bottom of the run to the west of the hut. "So the track should be just over there. If we take this up, we should hit it." The snow was starting to intensify. Cole fell in behind him.

■

Standing outside the hut after Brett and Cole left, Joel and Morgaan decided to try to catch up. Joel wanted to ski with his boy. That was why they'd come. He and his daughter followed the first ski track they saw, heading northwest from the back of the cabin but quickly concluded it couldn't have been Cole and Brett because too much snow had accumulated on it, indicating it hadn't been used that day. They returned to the hut after fifteen minutes. The next track they found was fresher. They climbed for about half a mile before bumping into the trio who were also staying at the hut and had gone out earlier. Those people said only that they had seen Brett and Cole skinning toward the saddle, by now just a short distance away. Joel and Morgaan continued their ascent in that direction, where they came to a small clearing. The track indicated someone had stopped there and begun a descent into sparse trees. They saw two ski tracks headed north, farther into the wilderness and in the opposite direction from where they'd come.

They'd now been looking for Brett and Cole for two hours. At 12:47 p.m. Joel snapped a pair of photos of Morgaan, smiling in a purple and pink jacket with the hood up. Behind her, what appeared to be Brett and Cole's tracks led down an almost flat pitch that gradually steepened as it continued out of view. Joel and Morgaan didn't know it at the time, but just beyond where they could see, the saddle rolled into an abrupt ravine entering Porcupine Gulch. Fifty-foot-tall spruce trees towered over the clearing, their branches caked by fresh powder.

It was now snowing harder. Joel knew from forecasts he had seen the day before their trip that the weather would likely deteriorate.

"Looks like they went this way," Morgaan said, staring at

Morgaan near the rim of Porcupine Gulch, with Brett
and Cole's tracks visible behind her.

the trenches. "Should we follow them?" She was still hoping
they could all ski together.

Joel, who had a black shovel strapped to his backpack,
blade up, as well as goggles to shield his eyes from the falling
snow, thought the route looked risky. It would take them
farther from the safety of the hut. He took out his compass
and oriented it with a map of the area. They were standing
at 11,600 feet. All he could see were trees and clouds.

"I don't think this is right," he said, visualizing the run described by D-Bone. He looked at his map and then back at the tracks. "It doesn't seem like it drops down to the cabin. I just don't feel comfortable doing it. Let's head back and see if we meet up with them there."

Morgaan, still curious, skied down just far enough to peer over the edge of the saddle. The tracks disappeared into a heavily treed gully. The route worried her because she couldn't see where it led, and she climbed back to her dad.

Joel was now irritated by the turn of events. His plan to spend time with Cole had crumbled. Still, he figured Brett knew where he was going, and they were strong. Maybe Brett had another route in mind that would lead back to the hut. Joel didn't want to chase after them with his daughter in a worsening storm. Cole was safe with Brett, who was experienced and a father himself. At least, he trusted that much.

Joel and Morgaan removed their skins to descend back toward the hut. Instead of following their track, they decided to make turns in the powder. But the pitch was too moderate, and the snow too deep, to maintain speed. After a short run they put their skins back on and returned to the hut, a slog that felt almost as strenuous as the climb.

Brooke and Melissa, meanwhile, had traveled just a couple hundred yards from Uncle Bud's on their cross-country skis before stopping. Brooke was used to her dad rushing off and thought little of it. She and Melissa returned to the hut and spent the next two hours making snow angels and building a fort and snowman off the front deck, while watching pretty flakes float down from the sky.

Chuck also turned around not far from the cabin because of pain in his ankle and shin, a result of not skiing much before the trip. He skinned back and went inside to take his boots off. Their plan to stick together had splintered.

When Joel and Morgaan returned to find the rest of their group at Uncle Bud's, it was almost 1:30—three hours after Brett and Cole had left. Joel asked if anyone had seen them. Nobody had. The snow was now coming down sideways.

—

Two o'clock, their meeting time for lunch, came and went. "Did your dad say what time he was going to be back?" Joel asked Brooke.

"He didn't tell me anything," she said. She thought it was odd that her father and Cole had been gone for so long. But she always returned to the most likely outcome: that they'd reappear and everyone would exhale. It would make that sense of something being off feel right again.

Chuck could sense the crew growing uneasy. But he chalked up Brett and Cole's absence to overzealousness— those two were simply having fun, unwilling to stop skiing powder. After all, it was Brett. Spending long days outside, even in harsh weather, was what he did for a living.

The wind had started to whistle.

Joel was the first to raise the idea that this day, which had seemed so ordinary—a day like dozens of others he had experienced at huts—could be getting dangerous. He said he might call 911 and initiate a search. Others persuaded him to hold off, lest they sound a false alarm. There is an unwritten code among adventurers not to request help before it's actually needed. "Just give them ten more minutes," Morgaan pleaded. "They'll show up."

Everyone kept looking out the window, expecting Brett and Cole to burst in from the forest.

—

As they continued traversing left, Cole's secondhand climbing skins kept falling off his secondhand skis, a pair of 181-centimeter K2 Coombacks popular among avid skiers. The glue was now frozen, and the metal hooks that attach to the tail were too loose to keep the skins in place on their own. He put the skins in his jacket to warm up the glue. (He considered using the duct tape his dad had wrapped around his poles—in case of emergency—as a means of anchoring the skins, but the tape was frozen too.)

The temperature was in the twenties. The plastic "fish scales" on Brett's skis, a textured pattern commonly found on the bottoms of cross-country skis to grip the snow, were useless in the mush, unable to gain purchase. The track back to the hut that they'd expected to find was nowhere to be seen. Brett suggested hiking straight uphill instead. So they clicked out of their bindings, shouldered their skis, and began wallowing.

The snow brushed their waists as Brett and Cole inched up the steep slope, one stunted step at a time. They had stopped traversing to their left a few hundred vertical feet below the saddle, a distance that felt attainable to climb. They took turns at the front, plowing through drifts until they could barely lift their legs. It felt like trying to climb out of a vat of sugar.

Eventually they placed their skis horizontally in front of their torsos and dug the edges into the snow, pulling with both hands as if rowing a boat, trying to drag themselves up the mountain. It made little difference.

How had they even gotten into this situation? This was not supposed to happen with something so straightforward—a quick loop from a hut known for its easy terrain. They were supposed to be back at the crackling fire, nestled with their families, eating afternoon snacks.

They stopped to rest. Cole, wearing a bigger pack than Brett, leaned into the slope, taking weight off his feet, which brought relief. Snow fell like tiny feathers. The sun's dull glow struggled to break through the clouds; the sky appeared to be getting darker. Wading through dry, bottomless snow had only bled their strength. They'd gained just thirty feet since they took off their skis and were already spent.

Neither would confess but both had started to feel the slow boil of panic. They didn't know much about winter survival; the basics, however, were clear: They were stuck in the wilderness with almost no supplies, their isolation compounded by deep snow. They couldn't stay here.

Maybe more surface area would keep them on top of the sugar. They clicked back into their bindings and began to side-step up the mountain. But even with their weight distributed across the length of the skis, they sank to their thighs. It began to feel pointless. They'd gone only another thirty feet.

The air was still, the forest quiet. But the terror crept in.

"*Fuck!*" Brett yelled at the ground. He was hunched over, exhausted.

Cole felt a jolt of fear radiate through him. He wanted to yell too; whatever was rising toward his throat would have to come out. But he worried about what might happen if he gave in to the urge. He clamped it down. For a moment it dissipated.

Brett's shout amplified the desperation in the air. Cole's thoughts grew more frantic. What clue had they missed? Where were they? How many hours had gone by? He started to make bargains in his mind—if they could escape this, he would live virtuously, sans vices. Whatever it took to survive.

They'd now been out for approximately four hours. In the distance, below and to their left, they spied an old ski track on what appeared to be a lower-angled slope, traveling from the gulch up toward the ridge. It looked like an easier way to gain the saddle, which would allow them to ski back to the hut. But it was difficult to tell. If they were to ski down there, they might find even tougher conditions. Both realized every vertical foot they lost would be one they must regain, and if they couldn't get back up, they might be trapped in the gulch, out of options.

They had little food and water, and no map to tell where they were. Normally Brett, a casual pot smoker, would've had a lighter, which they could have used to start a fire. But he had left his pot at home, not wanting to compromise his time with Brooke.

They talked about what to do for twenty minutes. Each option analyzed made them sigh. The only way out appeared to be up, yet sometimes in the mountains you have to give to gain. Brett felt their best choice was to descend. Cole had been reluc-

tant to voice his opinion before, but now, unnerved, he spoke up and agreed: Continuing to wallow was futile. They had to go down, keep moving so as not to freeze. Even if the choice was blind.

Their rationale was typical: Research shows that most people who are lost eventually go downhill.

Brett dropped in first, then Cole. They slashed S-turns down an open face lined by boulders, momentarily buoyed by a feeling that everything was okay, because powder skiing can do that. Upon reaching the bottom, however, they discovered the old track did not ascend a lower-angled slope, but an even steeper one. Whoever made it must have had better gear than they did now. Their spirits sank, as their anxiety spiked.

—

Joel and Chuck hadn't interacted much with the other trio at the hut, but around three o'clock, Joel asked the strangers to help with a search. Chuck's ankle and shin were throbbing from the prior day's ascent, and he could barely put on his boot, so he was out.

Snow dropped in sheets outside. This was their last hope before calling 911. They formed two groups and planned to meet back at the hut no later than 4 p.m., roughly an hour before it got dark. They would take avalanche rescue gear and stay in visual contact within their respective groups. Searching for any clue but especially ski tracks, Joel, Morgaan, and a man from the other party skied a few hundred feet below the hut in case Brett and Cole had missed it and continued down toward Turquoise Lake. Two of the man's friends retraced their route to the saddle.

Morgaan was shocked by how deep the snow had gotten in the ninety minutes she had been inside. Breaking trail was arduous, as if she were trudging through quicksand. She and her dad traded off at the front. Tall, bushy spruce trees spaced just six feet apart created a sense of enclosure, as if they were moving from one dark room to the next, unable to see between them. They yelled as they broke trail, hoping to catch Cole or Brett's ear, but the wind drowned out their shouts. They didn't know if they were looking for an avalanche debris field or wayward ski tracks leading to where Brett and Cole might be hunkered down, waiting for help.

By the time Joel and Morgaan turned around and started climbing back to the hut, their trail from a half hour earlier was nearly gone. The snow fell as heavily as a summer downpour, erasing any signs of human presence.

Brooke, meanwhile, had not gone out. She sat at the hut with Chuck and Melissa, waiting for her dad. Their joyful drive to the trailhead already seemed so much longer than a day ago. She couldn't hide her worry. "This is really weird," she said to Melissa. "Like, where are they?"

It was one thing for her dad to be frolicking on a beautiful day and forget to return—he often came home from an adventure later than planned—but not in the middle of a blizzard.

The search teams returned to the hut having found no trace

of Brett and Cole. The sheer mystery of their disappearance left little alternative but to summon help. Unlike when a person goes missing in an urban area, there is no minimum time one must wait before reporting a backcountry traveler overdue and requesting a search. Chuck called 911 at 4:50 p.m. A dispatcher alerted the Lake County Search and Rescue Team.

Brooke dialed her mom, not knowing if the call would go through. Cari, a nurse, had just gotten home from work. The blizzard raged in Salida, too. "We can't find Dad," Brooke said. Her tone betrayed her terror. Cari immediately sensed the seriousness of the situation. Brett liked to get away from civilization, but never had he failed to return.

Bari had spent the afternoon skiing at Monarch with friends. Near the end, she remembered her dad's birthday the next day. *Oh, no. I haven't gotten him anything*, she thought. She decided to handle it on his birthday itself, January 5, before he returned on Friday.

She went to swim practice at the Salida Hot Springs pool around 3 p.m. By the time she walked out that evening, she had twenty missed calls from her mom and a text message that read, "Call me right away."

Bari had always been an anxious kid. If Cari told her she was going to the store and would return by one o'clock, Bari waited until one, then took off running and screaming for her mom, sure that something bad had happened. She phoned Cari from the parking lot. After the call, she turned to her best friend and teammate, Abby Ceglowski, in tears. "I have to go right now. I have to go," she said. "They can't find my dad." She drove the mile home in a panic.

Back at Uncle Bud's, Brooke had tried to remain calm for long enough. Suddenly, with darkness encroaching, she gave in to a frantic urge. *I can't sit in this friggin' hut by myself anymore. I'm going to find him.* She put on her cross-country skis and heard someone shout, "Don't go too far" as she slipped out the door into the swirling storm. Terrified of avalanches and unsure what direction to look in the fading light, Brooke skied through powder up to her knees. It felt like she was plodding in slow motion, the way each step sucked so much strength from her legs. Snow billowed off the sagging tree branches. Somewhere, this forest was holding Brett and Cole. But where? And why couldn't they get back to the hut?

Twenty minutes later, Brooke accepted that her search was hopeless. Despair flooded her body. The trees muffled her screams. Windblown crystals raked her face. She had never felt so lonely.

She pushed back to the hut and tromped in sullen and demoralized. Morgaan went over and held her. "It's going to be okay," Morgaan said, with little conviction. They both cried.

The weather alone put Brett and Cole's survival at risk. Every body suffers hypothermia, or a significant drop in core temperature, differently. The first sign is shivering, but if someone remains exposed to cold for a long time, eventually the heart stops. How fast that happens depends on factors such as fitness, age, and air temperature. Without shelter, Brett and Cole had a limited time before moderate hypothermia would set in. Then the deterioration would accelerate.

—

Anita Mason was at home in her loft when she answered the call from Lake County Dispatch. A Denver native and retired Air Force mechanic, with short dark hair and brown eyes, the sixty-two-year-old Mason lived alone in a log cabin perched above the Village of Twin Lakes, a tiny community twenty miles south of Leadville. She was the on-call incident commander with Lake County Search and Rescue, or LCSAR. As in most counties throughout the West, the sheriff has statutory authority over search and rescue and relies on a team of local volunteers to carry out the mission. Mason could offer a soft smile, but she was self-sufficient and tough; once, when an army Black Hawk helicopter crashed on top of Mount Massive, killing four decorated members of the Night Stalkers special-operations regiment, Mason hiked up to 14,100 feet and spent the night guarding two corpses that remained in the ship.

She had built much of her house herself and, before joining LCSAR, helped organize the citizen's emergency response team in Twin Lakes—a mini-SAR unit that could respond quickly to calls originating near the twenty-three-person village. She had never married and had no kids. Some LCSAR members called her "Mom."

She didn't panic easily, and she spoke in blunt terms. Mason once took a call from a hiker who told her his knees hurt. "Well, you're climbing a fourteener," she said. "Everyone's knees hurt."

"You can't come get me with an ATV?"

"Sir, this isn't Disney World. I don't have a secret door. I can bring up horses or we can carry you down on a litter."

"I think I'll be okay." *Click.*

Lake County hadn't caught on as a backcountry ski destination yet, and hut trippers tended to be savvy and prepared, so winter missions were rare. More often than not, LCSAR's small team was adequate for its need.

This time the info Mason received was spotty but painted a basic picture: Two male hikers, ages fifteen and forty-seven, had become separated from their group shortly after 10 a.m. Both were in excellent physical shape, with no known allergies or medical conditions that might necessitate an emergent response. They were experienced in the backcountry; the man was a Forest Service employee from Salida. She was told they had water, snacks, a shovel, and a whistle—and that the adult had his pack with him, signaling a higher degree of preparation for the storm that was now pummeling the Sawatch Range.

That information, as well as the whiteout conditions, led Mason to conclude the team would likely wait until morning, then deploy if the pair hadn't returned. However, LCSAR also had tools to make that decision less subjective—chief among them the Search Urgency Chart, a SAR questionnaire developed in the 1970s by a National Park Service ranger named

Bill Wade. The chart was part of a course Wade taught to fellow rangers, tagline "Search is an emergency." Now utilized by SAR teams across the country, it assesses eleven categories and provides an overall score between 11 and 41; the lower the number, the more urgent the search. Some categories are concrete, like how many subjects there are, while others leave room for interpretation, like whether they're "at risk for any reason." Additional factors include the subjects' medical condition, physical condition, and experience. Most totals land in the middle range (16 to 27), which dictates a "measured response." Such was the case for Brett and Cole.

Since Wade created the chart, however, it had been modified to include a clause that could override the sum. If any of seven specified categories were to be rated a 1, "the search could require an urgent response." There were multiple potential 1's in Brett and Cole's predicament: "Inadequate or insufficient clothing," "existing hazardous weather," and "inadequate equipment for activity/environment." But LCSAR had never viewed the chart as a mandate or gospel, only as a guide. And the team had no reason to believe the subjects' clothing or equipment was inadequate.

Its volunteers usually landed on the same page. While busier, neighboring counties often got twenty or more members to respond to calls, LCSAR's core used an acronym to describe their response: STP, or same ten people. "In reality, it was more like 'same four people,'" John Holm, the team's longest tenured member, said. He worked as a chairlift mechanic at Copper Mountain, twenty-five miles north of Leadville, and sometimes scraped together missions by phone from the top of a lift tower because no one in Leadville was available to run incident command. Mountain-town transience depleted their ranks. The team used newspaper ads to recruit new members. "It basically said, 'We're looking for volunteers, unpaid, no experience necessary, we're just happy to have you,'" Holm said of the ad he answered in 2008.

Members grew close, training and recreating together between missions. "I think some of us didn't really want new members, because we got along so well and liked the core group we had," Jacqlyn DuCharme, who joined in 2014, said.

The problem was that, every so often, a mission came along that was bigger, more complex, and more difficult than what their team was designed to handle.

—

Cole and Brett had tried to ascend where they'd seen the track, walking straight up the fall line. Cole's skins failed first, slipping off his skis and causing him to slide backward. Brett's scales held for another few feet, then he slid back. The slope was too steep, the snow too dry, their strength too feeble.

Going up wouldn't work.

They retreated downhill again, but with no clear plan in mind. It at least felt better to do something that was physically possible. They wandered through the crepuscular forest in a daze, unsure what they were looking for beyond a miracle, like stumbling upon a hunter's cabin.

Cole noticed Brett wore only thin glove liners—adequate for the quick lap they had originally intended, but not for conditions like this. Cole had thicker gloves and a pair of mittens stuffed in his pack in case it got really cold or his gloves got wet. He dug down to find them and offered the mittens to Brett. "Hey, I brought these but my hands are fine right now. Do you want them?"

Brett accepted. "Thanks." He slipped them on, grateful for any warmth he could get, given his minimal clothing. While Cole had on insulated pants and a down jacket under a waterproof shell, Brett wore thin duct-taped pants and a light upper midlayer.

In their wandering, they eventually came to a small hill. Brett stopped. It was as good a place as any to try to build a shelter, he told Cole. They dug into the slope, forming a crater roughly eight feet in diameter and two feet deep. The snow was too dry to support a cave. Brett didn't say anything about spending the night, but Cole knew—this was their bed. The day's last light had given way to darkness. Neither was enthusiastic about the protection the crater afforded. But it was obvious they had no other choice. Brett took out a granola bar and gave Cole half. They bit into the cold, dry hunks and worked them into softer pieces to swallow. The temperature, though below freezing, remained bearable. Ethereal snow drifted through the still air. They lay in a spooning position, their bodies touching. Cole was the little spoon, cradled by Brett's larger frame. There was no fatherly reassurance—just two beings trying to survive.

As soon as Cari hung up the phone with Brooke, she contemplated what she could do from afar. Getting people out searching immediately was her best hope. *Brett needs to know that I'm trying to help*, she thought.

She called D-Bone first, the hutmaster who had shuttled in the group's packs the day before. He was one of many Salidans whom Brett had taken under his wing. Brett chose newcomers, or those down on their luck or lonely; he would treat them to lunch, invite them on a bike ride, drop by their house, or just call to check in. "If it was someone who was more in the community, he could be less enthusiastic about those people than the ones who needed him," explains Mike Reed. "But, also, he needed them. Because to them, he was their hero."

D-Bone didn't require the lift as much as some. He grew up in Birmingham, Alabama, "right around the corner from 'Dega," he says of the famous NASCAR track at Talladega. "I was always out fishin', huntin', fuckin' off on my bike." When he started skipping school to follow the band Phish at age fifteen, someone anointed him D-Bone. "And I have not been able to shake it," he says, in a way that suggests that is fine by him.

After graduating from Jacksonville State near Atlanta, D-Bone promptly embarked on what he calls "my transient life after school and whatnot." He hiked the nearly twenty-two-hundred-mile Appalachian Trail from Maine to Georgia in 2003. After a few months, he went back to repeat a short section near the southern terminus for fun. But he kept finding free food in hiker boxes, and, well, one week marveling at mountains and streams led to another. Soon enough he had finished the whole thing again. "I did that on an ounce of grass and five hundred bucks," he says proudly, having lived on a hundred dollars a month. After he got off the trail in September 2004, D-Bone drove out to visit some friends in Leadville. His Isuzu Trooper broke down in Kansas, and while kayaking to pass the time as it got fixed, someone burglarized the cabin where he was staying. He rolled into the Cloud City with sixty dollars to his name.

This was actually not that unusual for Leadville, one of the classic boom-bust towns in the West. Perched on a gentle hill at 10,158 feet, ringed by a sawtooth skyline, the city was settled by gold miners in 1859 and grew to thirty thousand residents by 1880, almost as large as Denver (Leadville briefly was considered for the state-capital designation). But the silver crash of 1893 and a string of other calamities, most tied to mining, drove people out. During the early 1940s, the army's newly formed 10th Mountain Division and its fourteen thousand soldiers, who were recruited to defeat Hitler in winter, took up residence at the hastily constructed Camp Hale and trained at Cooper Hill, a small ski area ten miles north of Leadville. The camp lasted for four years, but it was what happened after they left that changed the concept of mountain living.

Many of the former ski troopers went on to become ski instructors or patrollers or guides. Some started new resorts, like Aspen and Vail. Others manufactured gear. Together they helped launch what would become a multibillion-dollar outdoor industry, propping up cool towns across the country and providing jobs that paid people to spend their days outside. This was the life that Brett sought—and the ideal that would eventually be sold to mainstream America, through magazines and movies and national parks, as well as brands like Patagonia and the North Face that appealed to boulevardiers in Manhattan.

By the time D-Bone landed in Leadville, the population was down to a gritty twenty-seven hundred. "I was like, you know what you do when you're young and broke and need work?" D-Bone recalls. "Go blow your last sixty bucks at the bar and talk your way into a job." His plan worked; he ended up building log homes. Later he started a catering business. But he always had his eye on a different gig: working as a hutmaster for the 10th Mountain Division Hut Association.

D-Bone started shadowing hutmasters soon after he moved to town, spending full days in the field with no pay. After seven years, he finally scored a job. He saw it as career heaven: almost every morning he left the stress of the valley for an oasis in the clouds.

He met his future wife at the FIBArk whitewater festival in Salida, and they married in Leadville. They might have stayed forever if not for wanting to raise kids in a place with better educational options. "Once we started procreatin', we were like, we need to make the move," D-Bone says. "I love Leadville to death, it's where my heart is; just, the school systems aren't cuttin' it."

D-Bone moved to Salida in 2013, and a couple of days later, he noticed his shirtless, heavily tatted neighbor three houses down watering the grass and bumping Bob Marley on a travel speaker. Brett couldn't help but overhear D-Bone's tunes—he was playing Dark Star Orchestra, a popular Grateful Dead cover band, on his own speaker. D-Bone strolled over to introduce himself.

D-Bone, a new dad, admired how Brett balanced his life. They listened to music in Brett's shed after putting their kids to bed. Sometimes they stayed up late slamming beers, talking about nothing and everything at once. D-Bone never viewed himself as Brett's latest adopted soul; he just valued the friendship. "It was comforting, inviting," D-Bone says. "He made you feel like you're not just some gaper who moved to town. Because there's definitely some old-man-club shit in Salida."

When Cari called on the night of January 4, D-Bone had just gotten home from servicing the Eiseman Hut north of Vail—a two-hour drive from Salida, then another six miles and three thousand vertical feet on snow to the cabin. The storm had made his ski out harder, but the drive home was the most treacherous part because of the whiteout near Leadville. He was whupped. "Brett hasn't come back from skiing today," Cari said. "Is there anything we can do?"

D-Bone fielded those kinds of questions from time to time at huts, and he always told people the same thing: You need to call Search and Rescue. It could be sticky for the hut association to get involved, liability-wise, and searching for someone in a vast, snowy wilderness, like that which surrounded Uncle Bud's, was similar to trying to find a marble in an ocean. But D-Bone didn't tell Cari to call Search and Rescue. Instead, he said he could at least phone his colleague, Dave Lee, for a conditions update.

Cari pushed it. "Can you go up and look for him?" she asked. She had never been to Uncle Bud's, but she knew her request would place D-Bone in a raging blizzard at night and that alone carried significant risk.

D-Bone had three-year-old and six-month-old sons at home. If anyone else had requested he drive into a storm and start a search after dark, he would have said no. But he could tell that Cari was desperate. So he said yes.

The day before Brett left, he had walked over to D-Bone's house to discuss the trip. D-Bone gave him a guidebook and laid out a topographic map in his living room. He showed Brett the route to the hut and pointed out landmarks.

"Where's the good skiing?" Brett asked.

D-Bone traced a few easy runs on the map, including the mellow southeast lap bowl that dropped off Whiskey Knob—the most popular powder stash. Then he pointed to Porcupine Gulch and said, "This stuff back here is really steep and avalanche prone. Don't go there."

Brett was playing with D-Bone's sons during the conversation, and D-Bone later would doubt Brett grasped what he was trying to explain. "He was like, 'Oh, your kids are so cute, man!'" D-Bone says.

Before Brett left, D-Bone did one more thing. He knew Brett's skis were outdated. "Are you going to take those ancient things? Why don't you use these," he said, handing Brett his new pair. "They're like half the weight. It'll be fun." The skis, Voile Vector BCs, looked normal but were

specially designed for low-angle powder skiing: fat under-
foot to float on the surface, with scales on the plastic bottom
that allowed for faster laps, because you could climb without
skins. The only drawback was the scales were too shallow to
maintain grip on steep slopes or in deep, cohesionless snow.
In fact, the manufacturer's website includes a disclaimer that
states the "traction pattern does not eliminate the need to
carry skins." This was why D-Bone also loaned Brett skins.
(He gave him his avalanche transceiver as well, in case someone at the hut didn't have one. Brett ended up handing it to
Chuck the morning he and Cole left.)

Brett took the skis home that afternoon, grinning with
anticipation. "He was so amped," D-Bone recalls.

———

After getting off the phone with Cari, D-Bone called Dave Lee,
who had been working at the Skinner Hut six miles south of
Uncle Bud's and had returned home an hour earlier. Lee said
he and a colleague almost couldn't ride their snowmobile back
to their truck—on a flat road that is regularly groomed for
commercial dogsledding—because of how much fresh snow
there was. "Don't go up there," Lee said. "It's fucking gnarly;
we barely got out of Skinner. Call Search and Rescue and let
them deal with it. You know better."

"Yeah, but if this were you, I'd do the same thing," D-
Bone replied. Then he asked Lee, who'd been a hutmaster
for eleven years, if he could borrow the association's snowmobiles—1200cc utility machines.

Lee had just skied three miles down from Skinner, then snowmobiled another eight miles through what he estimated to be a foot of heavy snow. In better conditions, he would have rallied to join D-Bone. But not now. "You can't take the machines," Lee said. "If anything, they're gonna bog down and you'll get stuck before you get anywhere."

As gorgeous as deep powder is to recreate in, it also poses unique dangers. It can trap travelers, and in worst-case scenarios when people crash and land upside down, leaving them unable to right themselves, it can suffocate.

D-Bone had told Cari he wasn't going anywhere without Ed Trail, another close friend of Brett's and someone with whom D-Bone had hut tripped before. He left it to her to contact Trail. So that's who Cari called next.

Trail, forty-six, had a bushy brown beard, thick, hairy forearms, and an intense, wide-eyed stare. Locals knew him as one of the best snowmobilers in Salida. He and Brett had recreated together for years.

"Brett's been gone all day, we're worried about him," Cari said. "He doesn't have his phone. Can you go up there and look?"

"Absolutely," Trail replied.

He and D-Bone met at the Beasleys' house around six o'clock that evening, an hour after sunset. Trail drove from there, towing his snowmobile on a trailer. Because of the puking snow and lack of visibility, it was questionable whether they could even get to the trailhead, let alone snowmobile up to the hut and search the expansive backcountry around it.

D-Bone packed what he called his "oh shit kit"—a winter tent, sleeping bags, bivouac sacks, a gas stove, extra food and water, and plenty of hand warmers. If the sled got buried and they were stranded, at least they could hunker down. Trail brought everything he'd need to fix a broken snowmobile.

At Leadville Junction, seeking one more partner, D-Bone phoned his friend Jimmy Dalpes. Dalpes, a thirty-three-year-old firefighter, hunter, and skier, lived in Leadville and was intimately familiar with the backcountry around Uncle Bud's. He often traveled the Sawatch Range alone and carried extra survival gear on his adventures; D-Bone knew Dalpes could handle any situation they encountered, hence his listing in D-Bone's contacts: "Jimmy Motherfucking Dalpes."

"What are you doing right now?" D-Bone asked.

Dalpes, married and with an infant, was about to go to sleep. He'd been listening to the storm rage for hours, and D-Bone's plan alarmed him. "Daniel," he said, "we can't go up there right now. Being in those woods, at night, is just not safe."

"Well," D-Bone replied, "Brett is missing and no one's been able to contact him, so we're going."

Dalpes had hung out with Brett in Salida and knew immediately that something must have happened. He would join the search, but not until daylight for safety's sake. He agreed to meet at Leadville Junction at 6 a.m.; then he packed his gear and crawled into bed. As gusts rattled his windows, Dalpes couldn't shake a foreboding feeling. "It was almost like a higher power, going, *You need to get there as soon as possible*," he says.

—

The storm that was hammering central Colorado was not just any storm. It was what weather experts call an atmospheric river—massive streams of moisture that transport water from the tropics to the poles. Usually they travel over open oceans, but when they collide with land, the precipitation releases with ferocious intensity, creating floods and, in mountainous regions, high avalanche danger due to the enormous weight that the deluge places on a snowpack. Their impact is often surprisingly localized, considering the river stretches for thousands of miles. One watershed might see just moderate precipitation, while the next gets buried under multiple feet of snow.

Mike McHargue, Lake County's emergency manager and an incident commander with LCSAR, had been tracking the atmospheric river for days as it neared Colorado, studying radar and government forecasts. He knew that it held immense Pacific moisture and worried about Leadville losing power. He posted updates on social media warning residents to expect a whopper. Those warnings didn't reach Joel or Brett or Chuck, however, because they didn't subscribe to the page.

The river that hit January 4 was the first in a series of waves that would double the area's settled snow depth in eight days, from twenty-eight inches to fifty-six inches. But totals varied widely, even within Lake County, and it was impossible to know where the epicenter was.

As D-Bone and Trail rode Trail's snowmobile up Uncle

Bud's Road toward the hut—the final, steepest leg of the approach, after turning off Turquoise Lake Road—the amount of snow they plowed through astonished them. "A solid, true, three feet of freshies," Trail recalls. His machine had 180 horsepower and a top speed of 128 miles per hour. But it whined through hip-high drifts where the route was normally smooth and hardpacked—their first hint of what the backcountry might be like. *If we stop, we're fucked*, D-Bone recalls thinking as he clung to the bouncing sled in front of Trail, his backpack strapped to his chest. They couldn't see much, even with headlights on. Tree trunks whizzed by in a blur of flakes on the twisting corridor. Any miscalculation carried life-threatening consequences. D-Bone searched for landmarks that would tell him whether they were on course and called out directions as they went: "A little right!" "A little left!" It took three times as long as usual to cover six miles. They didn't see the hut until they almost collided with it.

—

The week before leaving for Uncle Bud's, Brett had bumped into Salida's district ranger, Jim Pitts, by the copy machine at the office. Pitts had two sons, one of whom played soccer with Cole, and he'd recently injured his back trying to keep up with his boys on dirt bikes. He had heard of Brett's upcoming outing and knew that Cole—young, fit, and fast—might push Brett similarly. He wanted to share the lesson he'd learned.

When Brett told him how excited he was about the trip,

Pitts said, "Well, just don't try to hang with a teenage boy."

Brett took offense to Pitts's comment. "Man, my girls are strong," he said, rattling off some of their accomplishments.

Pitts realized he had touched a nerve and tried to clarify. "I'm not taking that away from you, Brett. I'm just saying, it's a different intensity. There is something about a teenage boy and the relentless energy they have."

Brett looked at his boss. "Yeah. That's me."

Now, Cole and Brett shivered in their crater, backpacks placed over them for insulation. Time passed mostly in silence. Every hour or so, Brett roused them to march in place and keep the blood flowing. There were no jokes or banter; almost no words at all. Still, all would be okay if he could make it back to Brooke—and safely deliver Cole to Joel.

Brett had always thought it important to keep nature on his side, à la the bumper sticker plastered to his work truck: MAY THE FOREST BE WITH YOU. Now, though, it seemed to be against him.

Cole's mind began to drift in and out of lucidity, shifting between people and places as he huddled against Brett. Scenes from his childhood popped into his consciousness at random. He was sitting on his porch in summer. Then at the river, surrounded by faces from his youth. He replayed an eerie conversation he'd had in his friend Ben Fuller's garage two days before the hut trip, stemming from both of them having lost a parent. Fuller often built plywood BMX jumps at his family's campground in the San Juan Mountains. One day when he was twelve, his dad said he'd hit the jump if Ben hit it three times first. Ben landed all three, but when his dad went off, he didn't *carry enough speed. He crashed face first, paralyzing him from the neck down. He died two days later. Fuller, an only child, had struggled to move forward after the brutal loss.*

Sitting on Fuller's couch, the boys had talked about their grief—as well as how fortunate they were to have been raised in Salida. One of them posed a question: If you were to die today, would you be grateful for your life? Cole concluded he would be, mainly for the opportunities he was afforded and the people in it. But he would be angry that it ended so soon.

That sentiment resonated even stronger now. His mind seemed to be preparing for an end, which terrified him. I'm not ready to die. He thought about his dad and sister, surely worried beyond measure, and how he'd screwed up royally this time. The guilt of putting them in this position gnawed at him, especially so soon after his mother had died. At one point he thought he heard someone yell, and he stood up and shouted back, "Help! We're here!" Nobody responded.

The snow crunched under his and Brett's bodies any time one of them moved. Only thin layers of fabric separated their skin from the frozen ground. Blackness enveloped them.

—

D-Bone and Trail's arrival at 10 p.m. delivered hope to the hut. Simply hearing the front door open jolted everyone to attention. After a brief conversation with Joel and Chuck, D-Bone and Trail made a run back down to Turquoise Lake Road, three miles round trip, just in case Brett and Cole had heard the whine of their machine and found their track. But the only track they saw was their own.

They figured they'd be better off waiting until dawn to search further and returned to the hut. Trail sat in the common room and texted everyone he knew who might be able to help scour the area come morning. One of those texts, at 12:09 a.m., went to Chris Tracy, an avid snowmobiler who owned Currents restaurant on F Street. "We have been looking for the past three hours," Trail wrote. "Search and rescue is coming first thing in the morning. If you and your boys could make it let me know. Deep deep up here. Thanks man." Tracy had grown up in Sioux City, Iowa, moved to town in 2001, and met Brett soon after. "Brett was one of the reasons why you wanted to live in Salida," Tracy says. "Like, you wanted to be like Brett. You wanted to do the things that he did."

These events needed heroes like Brett to pull through. Joel knew a story of stupendous survival in conditions not unlike what was at hand. But even it had a mixed outcome. On February 8, 1995, Bill Reeves—husband of Mary Reeves, who became one of Joel's partners in his practice—survived a single-engine plane crash high in the Sangre de Cristo Range just southeast of Salida. Reeves's copilot, Wil Atkinson, also escaped the impact—they smashed into a frozen lake at 11,700 feet while transporting a murder victim's body to the small town of Cortez—but during their snowy hike out the next day, Atkinson lost a shoe and began to show signs of hypothermia, mumbling and fumbling. He told Reeves to keep going, Reeves said later. They separated just before dark. Reeves made it to rescuers the following morning, forty hours after the crash. Atkinson died from exposure.

Afterward, Reeves told his story often, including that he'd left Atkinson to save himself—an act that wrought terrible guilt. Some never forgave him for leaving his partner behind.

He knew if he hadn't left, however, he likely would've died too.

＿

By this point, two rescue missions were taking shape—a government response, triggered by Chuck's 911 call from the hut, and a civilian response, initiated by Cari.

Twelve hours after Brett and Cole disappeared, it remained unclear what supplies they had with them. So Joel and the others took an inventory of their belongings late that night to see what might be missing. It wasn't reassuring. They found Brett's hut backpack, a map, two headlamps, a warm pair of gloves, and—the crushing blow—two cell phones. Neither Brett nor Cole was inclined to take his phone on adventures, but in this case their decision significantly reduced their searchability. Chuck called Dispatch again to report the findings.

Anita Mason felt a wave of deflation when she heard they had gone off so ill prepared. "Everything changed at that point," she recalls. It knocked out any hope from her assessment six hours earlier that they might be equipped to weather the storm.

LCSAR had deployed in blizzards before, but without a target search area, the odds of stumbling upon someone in the dark were minuscule. The question of whether to send volunteers into the field on this night, or wait until morning, involved three people: Mason, Mike McHargue, and a Leadville lifer named Rod Fenske, who held the ultimate authority. Fenske, slightly built at sixty-two, had worked for the police department for 25 years before being elected Lake County Sheriff in 2011. Trained in winter survival by 10th Mountain Division veterans who took him camping in minus-25-degree temperatures, Fenske hunted, fished, and had hiked the trails around Uncle Bud's since it was built.

"What's the plan on this?" he asked McHargue over the phone.

McHargue had talked to Mason and told Fenske they were leaning toward waiting until morning to enter the field. Fenske agreed—deploying at night would put volunteers in too much danger.

At 11 p.m., Mason asked Dispatch to send a text to LCSAR members explaining the scenario. If Brett and Cole weren't back by 5 a.m., roughly nineteen hours from when they had left the hut, the team was to meet at its cache, or base, in Leadville at 6:00 to gear up.

Cole's sister Morgaan never had been very religious, but she found herself praying that night. *If there is something out there, hear me: You better not do this because it will destroy us. It will destroy me.* She had lost her mother seven months earlier. Now Cole?

Joel in his despair looked to the spirit of Laurie. Before she died, he'd told her he was going to try to keep communicating with her. "I think that's possible," she said. Now, summoning her seemed like his only hope. *Laurie, Cole needs help. If you can do anything to protect him and keep him safe, please do it. Please bring our son home.*

He didn't feel any reassurance, but he was perched on the precipice of a deep, dark hole. Calling on Laurie kept him from falling to the bottom.

Joel checked the thermometer outside and felt a tinge of relief. It was twenty-six degrees—subfreezing, but not nearly as cold as it could be. He knew hypothermia's clock was ticking and that if Brett and Cole had not taken shelter somewhere, every degree of warmth would help delay the progression.

Unfortunately, the mercury would soon start to plummet.

—

Back in Salida, Cari and Bari felt trapped—by the blizzard, by the distance, by the thought of Brett suffering while they had warmth. Cari tried to convince herself that Brett and Cole had found an abandoned cabin and hunkered down. Bari kept calling and texting her dad, longing for him to answer, knowing he wouldn't because, she assumed, he was somewhere so remote that there wasn't any service. All she wanted was to be at Uncle Bud's with Brooke. Instead, she and Cari went to their rooms and tried to sleep. Guilt wouldn't let them. They lay awake for hours, listening to the wind howl.

Seventy miles north, Brooke's hope had given way to sunken despair. She didn't verbalize it, but she felt a chest pain, like someone was stabbing her. She wanted to throw up. More than anything, she wished she were with her mother and sister instead of suffering alone. Deafening gusts tore through the forest like angry spirits, shaking the cabin. Brooke thought what everyone thought: *I can't believe they're out there right now.*

Joel couldn't stand still. One minute he leaned against the wall in the living room, then he moved to the kitchen, then back to the living room. He frequently went outside to yell and whistle, a sharp, piercing summons through his thumb and index finger that he used to call his dog, Chaco. "Hey! Brett! Cole!" His wife had died over a period of months. This was different. He felt stripped to the core of his being, like his world was caving in and he could do nothing but languish in paternal helplessness.

No one knew what to think, but the most logical theory was that Brett and Cole had been involved in an avalanche.

Joel wondered whether they were together. Were they hurt? Making it through the night? Why hadn't they told anyone they were leaving? He never would've let Cole go without him.

Eventually everyone else fell asleep. Brooke and Morgaan curled up on the cushions by the fire. Chuck and Melissa retreated upstairs. The hut was silent but for a clock. Joel listened to it tick, second by second, like a bomb.

—

Perhaps it was an anomaly, perhaps their position, nestled into the forest's belly: While the storm seethed at Uncle Bud's, conditions stayed calm in the crater. A few inches of snow. Light wind. Silence and peace—on the outside. Cole lay next to Brett in the dark, wondering what would become of them. Neither shared his thoughts; doing so could risk an emotional breakdown and the dissolution of whatever hope remained.

Cole felt extremely cold, but not yet dangerously so. He was more concerned by what he'd observed in Brett as the day had worn on: fatigue, low energy, slower movement—signals that indicated Brett was having a hard time keeping himself going, let alone caring for a boy. Cole concluded his best chance for survival was within. But he needed to believe he could save himself, and right now he didn't. His mom had always quashed his doubt. Shortly before she died, bedridden and beyond any possibility of continuance, she told him he would experience someday a change in his life. He would gain motivation and become more productive, drawing on untapped strength within. "You will reach your potential," she said.

He longed to talk to her now. He tried to clear his mind and direct all his energy toward her, emitting a frequency. By signaling desperation, he hoped he might receive something back—strength, guidance, or motivation to continue. Before long, he felt a presence. He could not tell who it was; there was no image or voice. Only that it was female.

The spirit vanished without indicating whether he would survive.

6
THIN LINES

Brett had escaped numerous brushes with peril, on both water and land. Puer aeternuses, notoriously fun loving and spontaneous, feel a certain gravitational tug when surrounded by rivers and mountains. That ends badly from time to time. During his last year of college, Brett watched a three-day rainstorm turn normally tranquil Wildcat Creek in Manhattan, Kansas, into a churning maw of whitewater— some fifteen feet higher than normal. Brett and three friends hopped in canoes and tried to run it, weaving between flooded trees and under bridges as bystanders yelled at them to stop. Two of his friends capsized and abandoned their boat just before it smashed into a concrete pylon; they barely made it to shore. "Thinking back, it was everything you shouldn't do," says Mike Potts, who shared a canoe with Brett that day.

Brett and Ed Trail with their dirt bikes in 2002.

Another time, in his early forties, while dirt biking at Big Bend near Salida, Brett crashed at high speed. The impact knocked him out. Cari was driving with the girls to the Denver airport, en route to Washington, DC, for a sightseeing trip, when she got a call from Ed Trail. Brett was in the hospital, concussed and disoriented. His arm was broken. Later that night, after he'd been discharged, he discovered his shirt stuck to his abdomen with dried blood. Closer analysis revealed a gaping hole where a brake lever had impaled him.

But a weeklong ramble down the Salt River in 2008 proved the most extreme. It was a Salida boys trip, the likes of which Brett had joined many times before. When their flotilla put in below Show Low, Arizona, in Navajo County, the Salt's level measured fifteen hundred cubic feet per second—perfectly manageable conditions on one of America's whitewater crucibles. Their entourage included Potts, Phoenix, a local painter named Buddha, and a three-hundred-pound bartender known as Big Ben, among others. Some were dads. A handful of them, including Brett, had run the Salt together in April 1998, reveling in blue skies, short-sleeve days, and clear water. That trip, a year after Rob Walmer's death, served as Brett's introduction to many Salidans who became friends for life.

Ten years later, their group mistakenly arrived two days early for their scheduled launch time and ended up waiting in the pouring rain while other parties began their trips. They spent their initial night in tents shivering at a commercial rafting outpost. It was the first week of March. "You guys might want to think about camping high," a guide advised. Overnight, with temperatures in the thirties, heavy snow and rain saturated the White Mountains, all of it draining into the Salt. Brett and his buddies woke to a rabid cauldron of chocolate milk, still rising. At camp the next day, the surging water forced them to move their tents in the middle of the night. It would peak at almost ten thousand cubic feet per second.

Most of the guys had prepared for possibly bitter conditions. Brett, however, already the leanest member of the trip, had brought no warm clothes—a mistake that led his friends to wonder whether he could even continue. "Cold was not a friend of that person," Dave Carter says. Naccarato, sharing a 13 ½-foot raft with Brett, asked why he wasn't more equipped.

"Last time I was down here, it was eighty and sunny the whole time," Brett replied. Naccarato gave Brett his extra fleece and layers, quietly irritated by his partner's lack of gear.

Each day, the group rose in rain, sleet, hail, or snow and shot down to their next camp, where they huddled around flotsam-fueled fire pans until their joints functioned again, too chilled even to hold a beer. "It was hard-core, combat boating," Carter says.

Most were used to running big water and dealing with mishaps—they called their group the Wrecking Crew—but the Salt's rapids left them gripped. Any flip carried serious consequences. The thunder of giant boulders underwater vibrated as they entered munchy holes, hoping to be spit out. Brett, a self-taught oarsman, spent much of his time on all fours, pushing down on Naccarato's raft to keep its nose in the waves, which leaped twelve feet above the troughs. Eventually he took turns rowing to stave off hypothermia.

Of the group's three flips that week, two happened back to back. The first, in Quartzite, the Salt's most dangerous rapid, resulted in Buddha being held underwater for what felt to his partners like five minutes. The second, in a smaller but no less turbulent wave, left two men swimming for their lives. Brett and Naccarato chased after one but couldn't catch up. By the time they reached him, a mile and a half downriver, the man could barely grab their raft. Hypothermia was turning him numb. If he'd been stuck in the water for much longer, he likely would have sunk.

But as the days passed, the water eventually began to

recede, leaving massive logs wedged in cracks in the rock, ten feet above the river—a reminder of nature's power and what they'd just survived. Toward the end the group came upon a couple in their seventies who had been surprised by the storm and stayed put for six days, unwilling to proceed and risk a flip on their own.

It's a fair question what drives someone to accept such peril, under the guise of a friendly outing. Most adventurers see the danger as an enrichment, not a hidden cost or blurring of innocence, and often it does enrich their experience. The survival story sucks us in for two reasons: because nature effects a formidable foe, and we can picture ourselves as the protagonists—often lustfully so.

The Wrecking Crew's experience on the Salt became legend—something they still talked about. It bound them together in a way that backyard barbecues and garage jam sessions could not. They viewed their close calls as simply part of the adventure, not what they were, if you looked more critically: a brush with family ruin.

—

Unlike his approach to recreation, Brett prepared for every possible contingency at work. After all, he was the safety officer for the Salida Ranger District, which has twenty-seven permanent employees and dozens more seasonals, and he had received a US Department of Agriculture Certificate of Merit for doing "an outstanding job" in the role. "Brett always preached safety," says Dani Cook, the first female member—and, later, first crew leader—of the multiagency dirt-bike team that Brett oversaw. Cook and her colleagues started their day with what's known as a "tailgate safety session," dissecting everything that could go wrong and how they would respond.

If something did happen—a broken bone in the backcountry, a volunteer who forgot to take their meds and collapsed—Brett knew exactly whom to call. "He and I helicoptered, like, six people out over the years, from Mount Shavano and other places," says Chris Bove, one of the deans of search and rescue in Chaffee County.

Still, Brett's personal adventures prompted less prep than his professional outings—perhaps because he viewed recreation as freedom. Not everyone noticed his penchant to wing it or considered such habits to be detrimental; part of his charm was his impulse. But Naccarato worked in fire. Risk management was his life, even when he was off the clock. He and his team had a saying: *Take a couple minutes to plan, instead of making a plan a minute.* "My whole thing is to prepare for eventualities," he says. "But Brett was not necessarily that way. He would just go do, and what he had, he had."

Brett treated the wilderness almost as a person; being kind to it mattered. Poor trail etiquette, like bikers widening a single-track trail to avoid a rock poking out from the dirt, crushed him. "He would start yelling, 'God damn!'" Naccarato recalls, about Brett's shift in mood. "Or he would get really quiet. He would change. Like, I could feel it."

His energy and enthusiasm drew countless people in, but for others it was too much, and nothing bothered Brett more than when someone didn't like him. Once, when a Forest Service colleague excluded him from her birthday party, Brett fixated on it for days, agonizing over ways to broaden his appeal. "We talked about it while fishing," his friend Brian Sutton recalls. "I told him, 'Dude, you care too much. You need to let go, because you're never going to be liked by *every*body.'

"He was like, 'Why didn't she invite me? I don't understand. What can I do differently?' It was important to him. He needed that. And honestly, the world would be better if more people had those traits"—of caring what others thought of them.

Brett couldn't bring himself to be punitive in his job. As Salida's popularity grew and more outsiders started using the land, he would hand out multiple warnings to the same offender—someone riding a dirt bike off trail on Marshall Pass, for instance—as a way of avoiding a citation. This didn't sit well with the local conservation group, but Brett stood by his strategy. The only ticket he ever wrote went to a man who had parked his camper directly behind a steel sign that barred him from doing so. (Brett held violators accountable, in part, through a program known as "throttle therapy": making them rehab the land they'd damaged by working in the dirt.)

He insisted on honesty and taught his girls to always tell

the truth, even when it was inconvenient. He once quit a longstanding poker game because he didn't like "lying to my friends."

"Dude, it's bluffing," Naccarato countered. "It's part of the game."

"Yeah, I just don't like it," Brett said. This principle, too, extended to nature.

One day while doing trail work in Cottonwood Creek, he found a tiny red arrowhead. Many people would have taken the Native American artifact home as a keepsake—illegal as that is. Brett instead placed it under a rock thirty feet off the trail, marked by a sprawling juniper tree shaped like a pumpkin. He checked on it every time he rode by, asking his partners to look the other way while he retrieved it. Then one day the arrowhead was gone.

Brett threw his arms in the air and walked around talking to himself, almost frantic. "It was right here! Nobody could've found it. Nobody could've found it. I only showed a few people!" Ultimately, he concluded that someone had betrayed his trust. He held his head in his hands, devastated.

Brett was used to enjoying free rein in the wild, without having to check his spontaneity or whims. Cari decided early on to let him go on his trips—whether for an afternoon or a week—which she knew he needed, while she stayed home with their girls. But as the seasons passed, that took a toll, not just on her ambition but also on their relationship.

At times she felt she had nothing to do but be a parent. Friends saw the quiet badass in her, a wise mountain mama who exuded grace and grit. Eventually she decided to take ownership of her happiness.

In 2007, a female co-worker expressed interest in forming a roller-derby team. Cari had grown up competing in synchronized swimming—her Kansas City team took part in the 1984 Olympic demonstration in Los Angeles—and she missed the bonds that a team provides. Never mind that she didn't know how to roller skate. She committed immediately.

The squad came to be known as the Ark Valley High Rollers. They taped off a track in the fairgrounds parking lot and practiced two nights a week until nine o'clock. On weekends they traveled to bouts around the state. Cari's absence at home not only had a symbolic effect—she was finally drawing a line, saying, *I'm going to live my life too!*— but a logistical one. With her out, Brett had to stay home with their girls.

Brett had never seen Cari (derby name: Queen LaBeatcha) with such confidence and purpose as a mom. Eventually derby sucked him in too. He volunteered as the penalty-box manager, calling himself Crusty Demon of Hurt. "It seemed like he wanted to be a part of her more," says her friend Kim Bouldin, aka Nacho Sleeze. "The change was very visible."

In 2015, four High Rollers including Bouldin organized a skate across America for charity, starting in Cocoa Beach, Florida, and ending in Santa Monica, California. Cari joined them from Tallahassee to New Orleans, a 390-mile, ten-day stretch (the entire journey lasted seventy-eight days). She and Bouldin took turns pushing a baby stroller on highway shoulders, the rear skater clinging to the pusher's waist as she squeezed the brake to slow their descents. Once, in Alabama, they veered into traffic to dodge a refrigerator door. "It was so asininely miserable the whole time," Bouldin says. "But I think of who I would want to be in a miserable situation with, and it's Cari. Because we will somehow just laugh our asses off." Cari was, in a sense, the anti–Freaker Boy.

Turning fifty can be scary for anyone, suggestive as it is of the end. But most people don't dread the milestone until it's about to happen. Brett started fretting when he was in his mid-forties. Having his age start with a "five" could only mean he was on his way out. "He was *stressing*," says Dani Cook, whom he called Danimal. "I think he just recognized the connotation. His daughters were going to graduate, he's working at the same district, riding the same trails. *What are we gonna do?*"

Ironically, his concern coincided with an unexpected counterweight. For years he had worried about his and Cari's relationship, lamenting their divergence in talks with friends. It didn't feel like the same love they'd had in their twenties. Both had changed, grown. He struggled to grasp what that meant. Was what was best for him, still best for her? Simply pondering the question scared him. Then one day his tone changed. Naccarato noticed it, as did Cook. Bari and Brooke were more self-sufficient, and Brett and Cari began to reconnect. They played disc golf in the evenings, talking and laughing for hours. Brett stopped inviting third wheels and focused on her. During a field work day on Mount Shavano in the fall of 2016, Cook detected a sparkle in Brett, as if his fortune had become clearer. "It was super special to see him light up with joy again," she says.

As the snowpack took shape in December 2016, Brett skied Monarch Pass any chance he got. One morning he joined Potts and Randy Mishmash, a former snowcat guide and avalanche forecaster who had lived in Salida since the 1980s, for a skin up a mellow zone called Snow Stake. Mishmash was part of Monarch's old guard. He'd climbed twenty-thousand-foot peaks in Peru, spent more than a decade on Chaffee County South's SAR team, and earned a reputation for making safe choices. As they geared up to start, Brett couldn't believe how full Mishmash's pack was. "What do you have in there?" he asked.

"You know," Mishmash said, "backcountry skiing is the No. 1 most dangerous sport out there. Not just because of avalanches, but also the weather. Humans aren't made to survive in frozen conditions."

Then he emptied the contents of his pack. Wedged among the toilet paper, avalanche rescue gear, mittens, hand warmers, food, and water was a rusty Campbell's soup can with a piece of rolled-up cardboard inside covered in wax. One of his SAR mentors, Chris Bove, who worked in construction, had borrowed the idea from Mexican tradesmen who used homemade candles to heat their lunches. The point wasn't just to stay warm; it was to survive when nature turned and hypothermia crept in. "This thing will burn for four hours if I need it to," Mishmash told Brett. He also carried a plastic jar stuffed with newspaper and lighters. The kit had stayed in his pack for twenty years, sealed and unused.

If Brett took any lesson from their exchange, he hadn't put it into practice by the time he met D-Bone for another ski day a few weeks later. D-Bone razzed Brett about his dinky Forest Service pack and keychain compass. "You have nothing with you, dude. Come on. I've got all kinds of shit at the house. Throw some ski straps in at least"—rubber tethers that could hold just about anything together. "Or bailing wire, in case your skins fail or a binding blows out." Brett flashed a sheepish smile, and they proceeded on their adventure without mentioning it again.

"If you complained to him about mosquitoes, he'd be like, 'No, I just think 'em away,'" Cari says. "He thought he could think things into fruition."

Brett, nevertheless, had a history of getting out of back-country pickles. He often came home with tales of rescuing stuck snowmobiles or devising some clever fix for a broken bicycle. One day, he and Naccarato were riding the Rainbow Trail, a popular dirt roller coaster south of town, when Brett gashed his rear tire's sidewall. He hadn't brought a spare tube and the slice was too big to patch. He taped a dollar bill to the inside of the rubber, then he and Naccarato spent forty-five minutes stuffing it with grass, until it supported him enough to pedal back to the trailhead.

—

On New Year's Eve, three days before Brett left for Uncle Bud's, he and Cari attended a potluck at the former First Baptist Church that their friends Kurt and Sheree Bedding-field had purchased and renamed A Church. Two hundred people attended, dancing and catching up, celebrating the holiday. Brett spent much of the night at the door, like a greeter. Kurt and Sheree were still considering turning the space from a community center into a fourplex for financial reasons. But they didn't want to change what it was, and neither did Brett. "Man, this is just what Salida needs," he told Kurt in the foyer. "A place where everybody can come together."

Brett and Cari lingered long after midnight, playing ping-pong until it was time to go home to their girls. They walked four blocks under an ocean of stars in the cold, holding hands the whole time. "Just feeling really happy," Cari recalls.

7
THE MISSION

Tyler Lehmann awoke to a ringing phone at 2:30 a.m. on January 5. If Chris Tracy was calling this late, something was up.

Tracy, who snowmobiled eighty days a year, had been phoning a short list of riders who he believed would be able to handle the conditions around Uncle Bud's. Lehmann happened to be in Hayden, a small town three hours north of Leadville, guiding snowmobile tours. Tracy explained that Brett was missing and he was planning to mount a search in the morning. Lehmann's heart sank. *Not Brett.*

Lehmann had grown up in Salida, gangly and unathletic, addicted to the outdoors. While other twelve-year-olds played football or basketball, Lehmann took solo backpacking trips. He was a wayward Monarch ski patroller when he met Brett in 2004—"just a kid off the grid," as he put it. Brett saw someone with potential who needed guidance (and, as it turned out, an email account, which Brett started for him). He hired Lehmann, then twenty-four, to his OHV crew. Lehmann had lost his dad suddenly when he was fourteen, and he came to view Brett as a father figure.

Lehmann worked as Brett's right-hand man for seven years. Brett even took him dirt biking in Utah. But they butted heads over certain management philosophies, and Lehmann's youthful, wild side eventually built a wedge between them. He had been meaning to reconcile with Brett when he answered Tracy's call.

Despite the late hour, Lehmann immediately woke up his boss in the bunkhouse where they were staying. "I'm out," Lehmann said.

His boss reminded him that they were guiding in the morning.

"Then I quit," Lehmann said. "Whatever. I'm out."

He left the lodge and walked into the storm, loaded his snowmobile on a trailer, and started driving to Leadville at twenty-five miles per hour, barely able to see the road.

Tracy also decided to put a request for help on Instagram. Brett hated social media and refused to participate. "I don't need that," he said. In this case, however, it seemed to Tracy like the quickest way to rally the masses. Before dawn, he posted a photo of Uncle Bud's with the word "Attention" scrawled across the bottom in red ink. "A local Salida resident and forest service agent Brett Beasley and a 14-year-old kid have been missing near uncle Bud's hut trip since 10:30 AM yesterday morning," Tracy wrote. "Search and rescue has been called. If any of my snowmobiling friends

●●●○○ Verizon 🅦   7:31 AM   ⓐ ✈ 99% ▰

‹   Photo   ↻

ctracy1
Salida, Colorado ›   •••

♡ ◯ ◁   ⊓

♥ 7 likes

ctracy1 Attention. A local Salida resident and forest
service agent Brett Beasley and a 14-year-old kid
have been missing near uncle Bud's hut trip since
10:30 AM yesterday morning. Search and rescue has
been called. If any of my snowmobiling friends has
knowledge of the area and can assist this morning
please direct message me. They are on skis only

55 MINUTES AGO

⌂   ◯   ⊕   ♡   ⚇

Chris Tracy's Instagram post.

has knowledge of the area and can assist this morning please direct message me. They are on skis only."

Naccarato, who had learned to snowmobile from Brett, saw Tracy's post when he woke. He called his boss, District Ranger Jim Pitts. "I'm taking the sleds," Naccarato said. "We're going to search for Brett."

Much of the town was preparing to ski Monarch that day.

Then an avalanche closed Monarch Pass, preventing the ski area from opening. The slide ripped through an aspen grove and flattened a stand of trees that had stood for decades above the road, signaling the fury at hand. People's phones started blasting. "Have you heard about Brett?" "Yeah, we're heading up to search." "Meet you up there."

The prior evening, after alerting D-Bone and Trail, Cari made one more fateful phone call to Brett's newest colleague, a firefighter with a thick brown beard named Dave McConathy. The forty-three-year-old Georgian had known Brett for only two months, but like a lot of new arrivals to Salida, they'd become fast friends. "It didn't matter if you were making him a peanut butter sandwich, the guy was happier'n a two-peckered puppy," McConathy says of Brett. Cari had heard them talk about snowmobiling and figured McConathy had connections. He was eating dinner at the bar at Currents when Cari called. To McConathy, she sounded terrified.

With good reason. If Brett and Cole were stuck in the storm, they had at that point been exposed for sixteen hours. The calculations were easy to make. It can take less than an hour to succumb to hypothermia in frigid temperatures— much colder than those at Uncle Bud's—but the longer the exposure, the more dangerous.

McConathy told Cari he would make some calls to see if other snowmobilers could help. The Arkansas Valley was full of talented riders, many of whom knew Brett personally. But only one was the king of his sport, and that's who McConathy called first. Chris Burandt, who backflipped over a one-hundred-foot gap to win an X Games gold medal in 2008, had moved to Buena Vista, halfway between Salida and Leadville, in 2016 to run Burandt's Backcountry Adventure, a popular guiding operation. McConathy met Burandt in the early 2000s. It had been ten years since they had last spoken.

Burandt, a thirty-eight-year-old father of two with an intense gaze and frenzied schedule, was driving home from a snowmobile dealer event in Denver. Brett had managed Burandt's permit with the Forest Service, a critical role to any outfitter. They had ridden together before, and Burandt knew Brett was a core moto guy—"one of us," he put it—which mattered as much as their professional relationship. When McConathy described the scenario, Burandt said, "I'll get the boys together and we'll be there first thing in the morning."

By that time, the storm was raging in Buena Vista, too. Burandt enlisted a capable wingman in twenty-four-year-old Chase Bunting, who lived at his house during the winter. Bunting was Burandt's top guide and something of a snowmobiling wunderkind. He'd grown up in Palisade, a farm town on Colorado's arid Western Slope, racing dirt bikes and snowboarding. He didn't touch a snowmobile until he was a sophomore in college. Then, at age twenty, he became obsessed with it. He repeatedly watched Burandt's riding segments from the old *Slednecks* movies as well as his YouTube catalog, learning everything from how to put a sled on edge to where to position his handlebars to how to feather the throttle with his thumb. During Bunting's senior year, he emailed Burandt through Burandt's website, offering eighty hours of free labor that he needed to complete for a course. When they finally rode together, Burandt was impressed. "Who taught you how to ride?" he said.

"You did," Bunting answered.

Burandt knocked on Bunting's door when it was still dark.

They left Burandt's compound shortly after dawn in a nuclear whiteout—snowfall so intense that it was hard to tell where the front field ended and the road began. Visibility was less than the length of a basketball court. They inched along at twenty miles per hour towing Burandt's trademark red, white, and black trailer, adorned with a giant photo of him smashing powder.

They converged on Leadville Junction maintaining a strangely nonurgent assumption. "Everybody kinda had this same view," Burandt recalls. "'Okay, Brett didn't make it back. Not a big deal. It's Brett. He's prepared; he can handle a situation.'" Brett, after all, was the snow ranger for a 440,000-acre swath of forest.

Among those coming to search, few even knew Cole was with him.

———

The cold in the crater never let Brett and Cole relax. They shook constantly, as if vibrating. Nearing the end of their thirteen hours of darkness, Cole finally fell asleep, his back still touching Brett's chest. He woke a half hour later. The first gray hints of dawn seeped into the forest. They decided to leave the crater and again attempt to ascend from where they'd seen the old track.

They skied up the slight incline one hundred yards to the base of the slope that they'd descended the day before, hoping a second try would yield different results. Maybe the snow would have consolidated, offering more grip. It looked daunting. They followed the faint track up, likely left over from a prior hut group's foray into Porcupine. Cole's skins slipped off almost immediately; the glue had not thawed enough to stick to his skis. He started sidestepping. Brett adopted Cole's approach. But the snow was still too soft and deep to justify the effort it took to complete each step.

Opting to preserve their energy, they turned around and once more headed down the gentle hill to where it flattened out. Cole's feet ached from the physical toll of constant movement. His skins dragged from his ski tips, unattached at the tail. Any optimism they'd felt at daybreak had given way, again, to panic.

Cole had committed to maintaining levelheadedness. Whatever was going to happen, he would accept. If that meant death, he just wanted to go in peace, not in the grip of terror. He had no idea where they were going. Or why it made sense to ski in this direction instead of another. Cole's pace had slowed. But not as much as Brett's. Brett seemed more lethargic than the previous day, quieter. The cold and exertion appeared to be grinding him down.

It was still painful to accept that their family outing had yielded this—a strain to simply stay alive.

—

So much snow had fallen after D-Bone and Trail got to Uncle Bud's that they couldn't even see Trail's snowmobile when they went outside to start it at 5 a.m. Almost every branch in the caked forest sagged under the weight of fresh powder. Snow continued to fall, but the gusts had subsided, leaving an eerie silence. Trail and D-Bone rode back down their track, now mostly filled in, to the parking lot six miles away, where they'd been instructed to meet Lake County Search and Rescue at sunrise. Jimmy Dalpes, D-Bone's friend from Leadville, was there, but LCSAR had not shown up yet. D-Bone felt as if he, Trail, and Dalpes demonstrated more urgency to find Brett and Cole than the official rescuers.

When the LCSAR contingent arrived around 7:30 a.m., in three vehicles, D-Bone noticed that some volunteers had brought snowshoes—a slower and less efficient mode of backcountry travel than skis. He and Trail had been waiting for more than an hour. "Ed and I were like, *let's go, let's go, let's go, let's go,*" D-Bone recalls.

He found a male team member whose name he now doesn't recall. "We're already at twenty hours" since Brett and Cole had left the hut; "we need to be moving," D-Bone told him. He knew hypothermia could kill people in far less time. Worried that the team would turn the parking lot into its base of operations instead of establishing one at the hut, D-Bone and Trail fired up their snowmobiles, which prompted the others to follow. D-Bone towed a pair of LCSAR members on skis up to the hut, where in front of the families he laid out a map and oriented everyone to the terrain. He also told the same male team member that highly skilled civilians would be coming from Salida, with powerful snowmobiles. Use them, he said. The man "kind of snickered," D-Bone recalls, as if doubting their necessity.

When the professionals, Burandt and Bunting, arrived, they met Tracy and two other expert sledders in the parking lot. By then Anita Mason had established a makeshift command out of her truck with radios and maps. But even the trailhead was a mess. A front-end loader clearing the lot got stuck in a ditch because the snow overwhelmed it, so the county called a second loader to pull out the first one.

The snowmobilers had looked over the maps. They chose Burandt as their leader and were ready to leave. When they approached Mason, however, she told them they were "not cleared to go on this search" because they weren't part of LCSAR's team. They took turns pleading their case, even mentioning Burandt's X Games gold medal, to no avail. The extraordinary asset of having the world's best backcountry snowmobiler to help would have to wait.

Burandt was annoyed, but he got it. Unprepared volunteers desperate to save loved ones can get in the way; SAR leaders can't evaluate everyone's skills individually on the fly, so it's easier for teams to draw a hard line. Left without a mission, the snowmobilers paced and shivered, griping under their breaths. Finally, Burandt approached Mason himself. "Can we please get up on the mountain and start looking?" he said. "I just need some details, as much information as you have." She explained that he would have to be able to communicate with LCSAR from the field, and the team wasn't in the habit of handing out its $3,000 radios to civilians—mostly because the radios required special training to operate.

Bunting knew exactly how to work the radio and told Mason as much. It was the same one he'd used at the Forest Service, where, over ten years, he had fought wildfires in six states, often via helicopter. Mason still said no. Only after Naccarato, an "agency guy," showed up in his green Forest Service uniform, offering a familiar face whom Mason had worked with before, did she begin to relent. She had no legal authority to prevent people from entering the field—like every SAR incident commander, she relied on the sheriff for enforcement—but Naccarato convinced her to trust the civilians. It was agreed that Burandt, Bunting, and Salida's sledders would proceed with Naccarato and his colleagues to the hut, then relay any findings from their search through Naccarato by radio.

Twenty-five years before being elected Lake County Sheriff in 2011 and trained in winter survival by 10th Mountain veterans who took him camping in minus-twenty-five-degree temperatures, Fenske like to hunt and fish and had hiked the trails around Uncle Bud's since it was built.

Though Rod Fenske showed up to LCSAR's bigger missions, he often sent his undersheriff or a deputy to less complicated outings. He viewed his role as one of support. If his office came into extra funding by way of a drug bust, he asked what the SAR team needed and ordered it. The arrangement was contingent on their acknowledging Fenske's top-dog status, however, and if someone challenged him, his outlook could change.

When Fenske arrived at bustling Leadville Junction on the morning of January 5, Lake County emergency manager Mike McHargue was about to leave for the hut to run the field operation. Five-foot-six with deep blue eyes, a round face, and two replaced hips, McHargue, fifty-seven, personified the rugged backcountry SAR guru. He had moved to Leadville after twenty years as an Army Ranger, quickly becoming a high-altitude anaerobic machine. Four times he earned "Leadman" distinction for finishing each of Leadville's toughest endurance races in a year, highlighted by the hundred-mile run and hundred-mile mountain bike ride on back-to-back weekends. He taught courses on active shooter response and lived for rescues. In the decade since he'd joined LCSAR, he had almost never missed a mission, usually responding to thirty or forty a year.

Few scenarios presented as ripe an opportunity for heroism as what had unfolded over the past day. The question was whether they could find Brett and Cole before it was too late—before nature slammed the door shut.

McHargue had rarely seen a storm like this one. That's one reason why he hadn't rushed volunteers into the field. Rescuers often face criticism for their measured response, but it stems from one of the most repeated phrases in SAR training: "Team comes first." The lost person had chosen to go out. The volunteers risked their own safety to help.

Missions sometimes attracted "spontaneous unaffiliated volunteers," or SUVs, as LCSAR members referred to civilians who showed up to search. They weren't always welcome because they could get in the way, but they'd proved their usefulness after the infamous 1962 Twin Lakes avalanche, one of the deadliest natural disasters in Colorado's history. Around 5:30 on Sunday morning, January 21, a mile-wide slab of snow broke free thousands of feet above Twin Lakes Village, high on the southern flank of Mount Elbert. An ocean of debris thundered down the mountain, swallowing four houses and trapping nine people. A family of five died, including ten- and seven-year-old sisters, as did two brothers from another family, ages seven and nine. A neighbor sounded the alarm three hours after the slide when he noticed the devastation out his window. Members of the nascent Lake County Rescue Team—LCSAR's precursor—rushed to the scene but quickly recognized the impossibility of searching a field that vast. Fortunately, scores of volunteers heard about the avalanche over the radio and joined the search. By early afternoon, 750 volunteers probed the debris. They pulled out two survivors, parents of the deceased boys, more than four hours after the accident. "The victims were found on their mattresses, covered by sheets and blankets as if they were still sleeping," the *Herald Democrat* reported. "The two little girls were found clutched in each other's arms." A pair of deer were suspected to have triggered the slide.

Mason knew that story from living in Twin Lakes, but LCSAR wasn't running a mile-wide grid search where every able body helped; it needed to determine where an expert outdoorsman and teenage boy had disappeared to during a routine ski outing. The fragile snowpack added a layer of danger to the search, which was why LCSAR requested a forecaster from the Colorado Avalanche Information Center (CAIC) to assist their mission that morning.

Blowing snow whipped around the trailhead, showing no sign of abating.

As more Salidans arrived at Leadville Junction—roughly twenty at this point—Mason's job got pricklier. She had completed multiday courses on how to manage staging zones and preserve a search area. But none of the hardmen wanted to hear he wasn't allowed to help, especially not from a sixty-two-year-old woman with crimson fingernails who walked with a limp. Fenske had left the parking lot by then, and Mason knew that vetting each SUV was unrealistic, so she told them, "If you'll just hang around here, I'll let you know if I need something." As people got fed up and self-deployed, any hope of accounting for who was in the field, and where they were, dissolved. The traditional system of managing a search—designed to prevent additional victims—had collapsed.

—

Two months before the hut trip, Brett had driven to Denver for a conference. His old friend from Kansas, Astro, took him to a Colorado Avalanche professional hockey game. In college, they had followed the Grateful Dead, and Astro considered Brett to be the older brother he didn't have.

Unlike Brett, Astro had taken the safe route in life, as an in-surance adjuster in the city. He knew Brett's penchant for adven-ture placed him in risky situations. On their way back to Brett's hotel after the game, Astro told a story about his sister's brother-in-law, Woody, with whom he'd attended high school. On Moth-er's Day 2015, Woody, his wife, and their three kids went for a family hike in the north Georgia hills outside Atlanta. Woody got separated at a fork in the trail and ended up trying to scale a small rock outcropping to reach his son, who had taken a slightly higher path. He lost his grip and fell backward, missed the ledge he'd been standing on, and tumbled down a steep incline, crush-ing his skull on a tree. His wife and children reached him shortly before he died. He was forty-three.

The accident shattered their kids, Astro explained, and he watched Brett process the story in disbelief. He had shared it to impress upon Brett the fragility of life and family, hoping it might resonate as he chased adventures. "That's how impor-tant each decision is," Astro told Brett. "Every step you take in nature, even tiny ones, can totally change everything. And you never know when."

Brett said what he always said: "Man, you're such a great friend. I love you."

"I love you too," Astro answered.

—

Because of the weight produced by the atmospheric river—the snow's average water content of 10.5 percent was nearly twice as dense as most storms that hit Colorado—the CAIC had issued a Special Avalanche Advisory at 8 a.m. on January 4, warning that the hazard was highest on north-facing slopes. The advisory ran through 10 a.m. the next day. "The new snow is not bonding well to the old snow surface," the forecast read. "If you trigger an avalanche in the new snow layers, the avalanche has the potential to step down to deeper weak layers resulting in a very large deadly avalanche." The January 5 forecast reiterated the peril, discouraging anyone from traveling in steep terrain. "A second wave of snow and strong winds arrives Thursday morning. This will only compound the increasingly dangerous mountain environment. Long-running avalanches could release naturally over the next 24 hours."

Everyone knew the danger of a slide and what Brett and Cole faced if they'd been involved in one. Most avalanche fatalities are caused by asphyxia, with trauma—people getting dragged through trees or over cliffs—being the second most common cause. But a victim often has a chance to escape before that happens. When caught in a moving mass of snow, experts recommend skiing at a forty-five-degree angle to try to get off a slab; barring that, "swimming," or fighting to avoid being sucked under the debris, can help prevent a burial. If those tactics are unsuccessful, creating an air pocket around your face is the best hope of buying time. As churning debris comes to a stop, it sets up like freshly poured concrete, preventing any movement whatsoever.

That's when time comes into play: A study published in *Nature* found that a buried victim has a 92 percent chance of survival if recovered within fifteen minutes. After thirty-five minutes, that chance drops to 30 percent. After 130 minutes, it plummets to 3 percent. Eventually hypothermia can kill if asphyxia doesn't.

One of the most commonly stated takeaways among avalanche survivors is that they underestimated the force involved, even in a small slide. Such is nature's power: impossible to comprehend until you feel it.

—

When Burandt and the other snowmobilers reached the hut, they were astonished by the amount of powder they found. Chris Tracy called it one of the two deepest days of his life. And the blizzard didn't seem to be letting up. Its second wave hammered them with unrelenting snow and wind. Inside the hut, the five Salidans felt they'd woken from a fever dream surrounded by walkie-talkies and hope. Brooke took comfort in seeing Naccarato and Trail, who had been like uncles to her. She believed them when they said they would find her dad. *It's still going to be okay*, she thought. Joel and Morgaan tried to muster similar optimism, but they worried how much more vulnerable Cole could be, since he didn't possess nearly as much experience as Brett.

The temperature kept dropping like lead. In town, it would fall forty-three degrees that day. Swings so drastic might feel routine in a place like Arizona, but in Leadville, it was almost unheard of.

The official search team had Joel's general description of

Brett and Cole's initial route, based upon their tracks at the saddle. But that information wasn't shared with everyone on the civilian team. Burandt remembered someone essentially gesturing toward the hut and saying, "That's where they skinned from." He had nothing else to go on.

Back home Burandt had waffled about what snowmobile to bring. He and Bunting always obsessed over sled builds, modifying them like mad scientists to achieve maximum power. Installing an aftermarket turbo engine could be a game-changer, increasing horsepower from 140 to upwards of 220 at high altitude. But turbos added twenty pounds and, like aircraft, required one-hundred-octane fuel to perform, what they called "race gas" instead of "pump gas." To reduce the overall weight, Bunting and Burandt would add ultralight aluminum tubing and carbon components. Burandt even replaced his steel bolts with titanium. If a cutting-edge sled cost $16,000 new, theirs came in between $40,000 and $50,000.

For this mission Burandt chose a stock machine with an extended chassis, in case he had to transport someone out of the wilderness. He and Bunting called it "Frankensled"—a freak. It was twelve feet long, a mix of black, gray, and lime, and looked like an aircraft carrier. It also had 30 percent less power than a turbo, and as soon as Burandt reached eleven thousand feet and saw how much fresh snow there was, he regretted his decision. He needed power. Bunting, meanwhile, had brought his shorter, race-gas turbo, which did ninety-five miles per hour on the flats.

LCSAR didn't have any snowmobiles in the same galaxy as Burandt's and Bunting's. John Holm, the team's sled buyer, usually opted for 600cc engines, an entry level (around eighty-five horsepower at altitude) that is common among government agencies. "I've always had the opinion that I don't want high-powered ones on the team," Holm says, "because not everyone can ride them and we may get in more trouble than our subjects."

As the defiant whine of bogged-down engines echoed through the forest, D-Bone and Dalpes formed a foursome on skis with CAIC forecaster Jason Konigsberg and LCSAR member Ryan Gab. Konigsberg would help them safely navigate avalanche terrain. Gab, twenty-nine, was a supervisor at Climax and one of the team's top skiers. Tall and barrel chested, with a dark buzz cut and easy grin, he had grown up in Kansas three hours from Brett, rooting for Kansas State. He learned to ski at Monarch during church trips. LCSAR had recruited him from Climax's mine rescue team two years earlier, and Gab (pronounced Gob) held training in rope, hazmat, avalanche, and swiftwater scenarios. Two children younger than five waited for him at home. He had learned to treat death on search and rescue as part of the job.

The four of them agreed by radio to meet Joel at the saddle where he'd seen Brett and Cole's tracks the day before. Although the mile-long climb rose only four hundred vertical feet, mildly undulating like a cornfield, Joel could barely make it. He had faded by the time he reached the top. His lack of energy perplexed him. *Am I really that out of shape?* Sweat soaked through his jacket. "This is the last place we saw their tracks," Joel told D-Bone, pointing downhill.

"Oh, they went into Porcupine Gulch," Gab replied. "We've seen people make that mistake before."

It was a mistake that could be fixed. The last time LCSAR rescued someone from Porcupine Gulch, a few years earlier, four team members spent an entire Christmas night searching for two skiers in a blizzard. The pair, a man and woman visiting from Hawaii, got lost traveling between huts and used a cell phone to call for help, fearing they wouldn't make it through the night. The call gave searchers a general idea of their location. McHargue and his twenty-two-year-old son, Nick, set out on snowshoes from Uncle Bud's while Holm and another volunteer checked known routes on snowmobiles. "We thought those people were gonna die," McHargue says. "That's why we went out." Mike and Nick heard the terrifying *whumpf* of snow collapsing as they descended into the gulch in the dark, dead reckoning toward the duo's location. They searched the forest until 4 a.m., whistling and yelling. Then they dug a trench and crawled in to sleep for a couple of hours, insulated by down jackets and down pants and a bivouac that kept the storm out.

At dawn, they climbed to a higher vantage point and spotted the couple below them, hunkered down on a knoll. Mike and Nick had been within a hundred yards of their location, but the subjects were asleep in their bags and never heard them. The sky by that time had cleared, and Mike requested a OH-58 Kiowa from the Colorado Army National Guard's High Altitude Aviation Training Site in Eagle, fifty miles northwest. The ship plucked the pair from the gulch and flew them out.

Now Cole and Brett's tracks offered the best clue for the rescuers on skis to find them. As they began heading in the same direction, Joel knew what was next—a question he dreaded.

"Do you want to come along?"

Joel hadn't slept since Tuesday night, and he didn't think he had enough fuel for the day. He'd planned only to mark where Brett and Cole had gone. If he dropped down the steep slope and was out all afternoon, would he be able to keep up? His fear for his son was countered by thoughts of Morgaan, who needed him at the hut. The question paralyzed him.

"I don't know," he said finally. "I feel like I could be more of a liability than a benefit, even though I have some medical knowledge. I think you guys will move faster without me."

He would second-guess his decision, but D-Bone breathed a sigh of relief. "Good call," he said, quietly grateful not to have to account for the liability.

Dalpes turned to D-Bone. He knew the hell on earth that loomed below. "They're in Porcupine," he said. "If their tracks went down there, there's no way they got out."

—

Brett's friends weren't the only ones who had seen Chris Tracy's Instagram post. So had Cari's friends. Samantha Bahn and Deb Bass-O'Brien immediately went to her house. They found her curled in a ball on the living-room floor next to her phone. She answered any question with "I don't know,

I don't know." At the time, because of Tracy's mention of a teenager, they assumed Brooke was the one lost in the storm with Brett. A lot of Salidans thought the same. They would learn the truth once word spread from the trailhead.

Bari felt frustrated just waiting at home. She had recently joined Leadville's high school Nordic ski team, because Salida didn't have one. She was an expert alpine skier and had helped Salida win three cross-country state titles as a runner. She begged to go search, but no one would let her. She and Cari spent the morning pacing, sitting, taking phone calls from Brooke and from bystanders at Leadville Junction. A friend dropped coffee on their porch, afraid to face them.

Across Salida, as the wind shrieked that day, the community came to a halt. Some meditated and prayed. Others stared at their phones. Ben Fuller kept texting Cole words of encouragement. Abby Ceglowski, Bari's best friend, sat in her car with Bari in front of the Beasleys' house and cried with her, still convinced her dad would be fine—if for no other reason than because of who he was. "There's no such thing as Salida without Brett," she said.

—

Cole tried not to think about how hungry he was, how thirsty, how cold. He'd watched movies about people trapped high on Everest. Emotions hinder progress, he knew. But for someone who had grown up in the mountains, he had no clue how to survive such a desolate scenario. Perhaps the smartest move he and Brett made was deciding not to eat snow—a counterintuitive act of desperation that uses more energy than it delivers.

Above the creek, which crept through the forest, icicles clung to downed trees. Thirty hours from now, this water would reach Salida. Not that it mattered. They might as well have been adrift in the Pacific, their environment felt so impossibly vast. The storm prevented them from seeing any landmarks. They discussed possible solutions to their situation: following the creek until they hit an open valley, where they hoped someone might see them from the ridge or a helicopter, if the weather allowed for a rescue flight.

They hadn't thought much of hypothermia, mostly because they had no control over it. When an animal is exposed to cold for a long period, it takes steps to defend its core temperature. Some, like hibernators and rodents, generate heat internally, without muscle activity, through a process called nonshivering thermogenesis. The rest of us, however, rely on involuntary shivering. Simultaneously, peripheral vasoconstriction, or a tightening of one's blood vessels, preserves heat. Shivering uses five times as much energy as sitting still, but it has been shown to dramatically slow the onset of severe hypothermia, where exposure becomes fatal.

The problem with shivering is that eventually it stops. That's when physiology comes into play: Fat people preserve body heat substantially better than skinny people. Brett was so lean he had veins popping out of his calves. Cole was less ripped but no more insulated. In the absence of natural insulation, a person's only tool to delay the progression of hypothermia is through voluntary exertion, like running in place. Or, *in their case, skiing down a desolate drainage, unsure where it might end.*

—

Though the howling wind had turned into a whisper in places, visibility remained low. McHargue knew that continued snowfall and misty air made aviation aid—including infrared technology, a critical SAR tool in missions like these—unlikely. A helicopter would have to fly beneath the ceiling but above the trees, a dangerous needle to thread. Still, McHargue asked again. "I need everything you can possibly give me," he said to his regional field manager with the state.

"I can't give you anything," the manager replied—the conditions were still too harsh. They couldn't even launch a drone.

McHargue wished he had a location. It was rare to not be able to ping a subject's cell phone (most phones send out a signal every thirty seconds, which nearby towers use to determine where the signal is strongest and thus which tower will deliver incoming calls). Normally he called Tyndall Air Force Base in Florida and asked them to triangulate a signal. This narrowed down the search area. Without that guide, volunteers at Uncle Bud's had no option but to blindly scour the ground.

A dense forest can't be searched both finely and fast. A three-mile radius—the distance from the hut to the lower reaches of Porcupine Gulch—includes 113 segments of 160 acres. In such vastness, a searcher almost has to trip over someone to find them.

D-Bone's team as well as Burandt's scoured the gladed lap bowl southeast of the saddle, looking for divots from old tracks, broken branches, any clue that might signify a person had been there. Porpoising through the deep snow choked the snowmobilers' throats and throttles. The fifteen-degree air burned their faces. Their sleds left trenches four feet deep; sometimes all they could see was white. On slanted sidehills, Tracy, who was riding a turbo last in line, had to get off his machine and cut a trail with his boots to maintain his course and not fall down the mountain. Naccarato's sled got stuck closer to the hut. He dismounted to dig himself out, and promptly sank to his chest. He had to belly-crawl like a seal in order to move.

What was usually a sublime endeavor—freeriding plush powder—unfolded as a practical nightmare.

At one point Burandt's group and D-Bone's group stopped on the saddle above Porcupine Gulch, out of sight of each other. Burandt and Bunting told the other sledders they were going to poke over the edge, hoping to see into the gulch. "You guys stay on this high point and be our radio relay," Burandt said. He turned to Bunting. "If we're going to be beneficial, we have to go."

Bunting nodded.

They knew that the others were only slowing them down.

By now most of the foot searchers not in D-Bone's group had returned to the hut. McHargue was coordinating comms, talking to people on three channels, relaying updates to Mason at the trailhead where she served as incident command. Morale inside Uncle Bud's was scant. None of the updates brought good news. The odds of a happy outcome seemed to drop by the minute. When McHargue and Naccarato started going outside to talk, Joel took it as a bad sign. He told Chuck, "I don't know if I can pull through this if Cole doesn't come back." It was the first time he'd verbalized his worst fear.

Chuck had been watching for signs of "wildness" in his friend—a loss of emotional control, like the situation could not be borne. Joel's comment alarmed him. Chuck didn't know what Joel would do, but he had been close to people who had ended their lives before, and he knew he couldn't predict it.

"You're going to come and live with us," Chuck said softly. "You're not going to be staying in that house by yourself." He, too, had to account for what now seemed a realistic possibility.

Chuck had been monitoring Brooke as well, checking in periodically. She mostly stared at the floor or into the fire. She had been using Cole's phone to call her mother, since her phone was dead. She didn't know his password, so she held the speaker to her mouth and spoke, dialing Cari's number with her voice, digit by digit. Chuck still assumed Brett would pull through, simply because he was Brett. He took Melissa aside. "Here's your role right now," he told her. "You're going to hang with Brooke; you don't have to do anything else. Just be with her. And if she needs space, give it to her. You can keep an eye on her for me, because this is going to be terrifying." Morgaan, the oldest kid at the hut, for the moment managed to stay calm.

—

Late that morning, Tyler Lehmann finally got to Leadville Junction. He had been driving for seven hours, through the darkness and into the bleak morning paste, panicked by the thought of Brett lost in the blizzard. D-Bone had given Lehmann's name to LCSAR that morning, as far as trustworthy people who could help. But when Lehmann, a professional guide trained in high-angle rescue, started unloading his snowmobile, a sheriff's deputy approached. "Sorry, we can't have anybody else go up," the deputy declared.

Lehmann was working on an hour and a half of sleep. He stood six-foot-five and weighed 230 pounds, and he hadn't come this far to back down. "Well, I'm going," he said and continued unstrapping his machine.

"Don't make me do something drastic," the deputy responded. "I don't want to arrest you." Lehmann stopped. As much as he ached to save his friend, and as livid as he felt standing there, he knew any further resistance would only yield trouble.

He left the parking lot and drove home.

Not long after, Mason posted a notice on LCSAR's Facebook page. "Lake County Search and Rescue has been dispatched to search for two lost individuals. We implore you to not attempt to provide aid in these endeavors, especially if you do not contact incident command first. The team has enough manpower currently and any more assistance may hinder or detract from current search efforts. Do not become another victim."

—

Brett and Cole followed the creek's indentation for a while, drifting away when the trees grew too thick. Three or four hours had passed since they'd quit trying to ascend. They didn't know where the creek would lead, only that the route offered less resistance than climbing. It was nearing midday. Their posture betrayed their exhaustion: hunched over and stiff, dragging each step as if limping. Cole had purposely stayed close to Brett, moving slower than he could have, afraid to pull away because of what it might portend. His mind raced.

Finally, he decided to go. But only for a short while. He stopped and waited for Brett to catch up. Once Brett did, Cole took off again. Then, once more, wracked by guilt, he stopped. The first time it took Brett five minutes to reach him. The second time, ten. Neither said much. At this point there was nothing to say.

Tiny crystals wafted down from above; the storm was abating. Cole had no idea if they were heading in the right direction, or if there was a right direction. Throughout his childhood, he'd been taught to respect nature, especially water. "River fucking kills," old-timers would say. He had felt the Ark's force first-hand, ejected from a raft and trapped in a hole, desperate for air. But the thing about cold is you can't get away from it. The forest, calm and hushed, was squeezing the life out of them like a python, twisting around as it slowly tightened its grip.

It's impossible to know what either of their core tempera-tures—or internal organ readings, which can be a couple of degrees warmer than skin-level measurements taken from, say, an armpit—was during this time. But hypothermia's effects often clue us in. Mental ability starts to noticeably decline at a core temp of 91.4 degrees. Shivering drops off at 89.6. A per-son loses consciousness at 86. The risk of cardiac arrest spikes starting at 82.4, where moderate hypothermia becomes severe hypothermia. The slope is slippery, and the process accelerates with age: Research has found that older men lose heat faster than younger men, starting at age forty-five. Brett was turning forty-seven at 8:30 p.m. that very day.

Another surge of exertion brought Cole to a small meadow, and he stopped again. He waited for fifteen minutes. Twenty, as his damp inner layers grew cold. For the first time, he won-dered whether this was where he would die. He gazed out upon a white field ringed by dark trees. There are definitely worse places to go, he concluded.

Behind Cole, following his track, Brett summoned every twitch of strength to continue shuffling forward.

Ten more minutes passed. Cole debated whether to go back and find Brett. Doing so would cost energy. He also knew, somewhere in his subconscious, that if he discovered Brett im-mobile, he would not leave him. Being in the same house when his mother died had traumatized him. He didn't know if he could face that again—watching someone die. Watching some-one's dad die.

Ultimately, Cole decided to wait. He sat down in the tran-

quil meadow. Whenever he elected to start moving again, he would walk until someone found him or until he fell over, he told himself.

———

As Burandt and Bunting cautiously entered Porcupine Gulch, separated by about fifty yards for safety purposes, suddenly it felt as if their sleds could sink to the ground. They descended slowly, not wanting to gain more speed than they could control. Then, almost simultaneously, both got stuck. Burandt was perched on a shelf—like a landing between steep flights of stairs. Below him, a cliff-strewn slope plunged into the densely treed gulch. He knew that if he rode any lower, he wouldn't be able to reverse course, because the incline was too sharp. So he did something he almost never had to do: took out his shovel and started digging a road back up to his track.

"Do not come down here!" he radioed to the ridge. "I don't think I'm getting out." They were a mile and a half from the hut.

His protégé Bunting was digging his own road above. The snow felt touchy around them, like a house of cards that could collapse at any moment. They wore airbag backpacks designed to keep them on top of an avalanche, but if the debris dragged them through thick timber, the bags would be shredded. Frustrated and unnerved by his position, Burandt stared into the shaded void below. He stopped digging. "Hey!" he yelled.

No answer. He kept digging. Then he yelled again. "Heyyyyyy!"

This time, to his astonishment, someone yelled back.

"Where are you?" the voice said.

Burandt felt a rush of excitement—and confusion. *Why are they asking me where* I *am?*

It didn't matter. It had to be Brett. The voice sounded like it was coming from the flats a few hundred yards away. Suddenly everything made sense: Brett and Cole had skied down and gotten stuck, then couldn't get back out. Most people keep going down when they get in trouble.

Burandt knew one thing for sure: If he descended the heavily loaded face he was looking at, there was no chance he was coming back up. He checked a topographic mapping app for potential escape routes, evaluating their viability by grade—the less steep, the better. If the weather were clear, they would've been able to see Highway 24 and the Tennessee Flats, a broad, open valley five miles east. His phone indicated that the mouth of Porcupine Gulch, below and to their right, would take them there.

He radioed Bunting, who was almost unstuck. "Get on my track and follow me down. I hear somebody yelling at me from below."

D-Bone's group, meanwhile, had begun picking their way down from the saddle, a half mile west of Burandt. They hadn't heard the snowmobiles' whine for a while, but they didn't realize that was because Burandt and Bunting were digging. The air was almost still. D-Bone looked to his left and saw a lynx, one of the most elusive creatures in the country, dart across the snow like a kitten on carpet.

They shouted into the abyss. "Brett!"

Silence.

Suddenly they heard a scream. They looked at each other wide-eyed. D-Bone and Dalpes thought it sounded like a dying war cry, coming from the gulch.

"Where are you?" D-Bone shouted back. He received no answer, but a minute later, he heard snowmobiles to his right, farther east. It sounded like the machines were descending.

Gab called McHargue on the radio at 12:16 p.m. "Hey, we've got voices. I don't know if it's the sledders or somebody else, but we've got some sort of contact here."

THE MISSION

8
THE CURSE

Sitting at the hut, Chuck couldn't believe it was happening again—a dire scenario involving kids and parents from Salida, detonating in his midst like a grenade. At the same time, however, he thought: *You've trained all your life for this. Just respond.*

Chuck wasn't only the principal of Longfellow Elementary. He often sat with young moms and dads who came to his office seeking advice on how to parent. Two families told him the reason they moved to Salida was because they had met him. Another local father called him "the most famous person in town." Slightly built with a gentle hunch, Chuck had dark blue eyes that twinkled, a warm smile like Robin Williams, and salt-and-pepper hair. He never had time but always had time—especially for adolescents who were struggling.

Chuck's father, an FBI agent, had encouraged Chuck to

enter the bureau after college, touting its pension and security. Instead, Chuck became a teacher. In his mid-twenties, he had wanted to find the consciousness that he had felt on LSD, but without taking drugs. So he started hanging out with monks.

He entered St. Benedict's Monastery in Snowmass, Colorado, a nontraditional place that allowed him to play music—his taste ran to Lynyrd Skynyrd and the Grateful Dead. He had to shed his belongings. He gave away eight guitars, including a Les Paul, but kept a pair of skis. For the first six months he cleaned toilets and mopped floors. He couldn't talk to anyone outside the monastery.

In the beginning that didn't bother him. Chuck felt at home among mystical cowboys. He skied from his front door and helped maintain the monastery's thirty-six-hundred-acre ranch, which included a bookstore, bakery, and retreat center.

The life had its challenges, however. "Silence makes it so the only thing you deal with is you," he says. "You're going through feelings and memories and your head's spinning, and you're miserable. It's the whole idea of how hard we are on ourselves."

Chuck also delved into dreamwork with a Jungian psychiatrist. A particular dream tortured him: He stood outside a monastery watching his brother, plastic tube in mouth, get buried alive by dirt. They interpreted it as a question: Was Chuck willing to bury his desire to help others if he professed for life? He couldn't counsel kids, his abbot, Joseph, told him. He couldn't even have a conversation with another monk unless he made an appointment.

One day Joseph confided that he saw Chuck as the next abbot—a post higher than bishop in the Catholic hierarchy. "This will all be yours," Joseph said.

It still wasn't enough to stay. In 1990, after four years, Chuck left the monastery. He was thirty-six. In the parlance of monks, he was "a failure." But no monk who left St. Benedict's had ever upheld warm relationships with those who remained, and Chuck did. He got married four years later and returned to education. In 2013 he became Longfellow's principal in Salida.

Chuck sometimes lamented what he'd given up at St. Benedict's—a kingdom at nine thousand feet, decades of penance and service to come. But as the famous Trappist abbot Thomas Keating reassured him afterward, "You'll be fine. Some of the best monks aren't in monasteries."

He might never know until he was in the moment when he would be needed.

The parent deaths had hit Salida so hard and fast that even those who lived through the nightmare forgot the order. Four in twenty-two months. Seven in twelve years—including six with daughters in the same friend group.

Everyone remembers the first, however.

Dave and Karen Adamson moved to Salida in 1996 from Denver. He was an anesthesiologist and a rabid outdoorsman who loved backpacking—hiking into a stunning location and camping under the stars. Karen, petite with striking green eyes and brown hair, was a SoCal mall girl and ICU nurse. Dave introduced her to the mountain life. While he finished residency in Denver, they drove around Colorado every weekend looking for a small town where they could raise a family. Salida captured their hearts. They sold their car and bought a little house on F Street. Their son, Jake, was one year old.

Dave started his own practice. They had a daughter, Jess, two years after Jake. Life was full and happy and just getting started. "Let's work part time until the kids don't like us anymore," Dave used to joke, "and then we can work more and save for their college education." He handled surgeries for every physician in town, sometimes missing his kids' birthdays, so he quit and took what's known as locum work, completing intense temporary contracts in rural areas around the West. "He was uber dad when he was home," Karen says. "Took the kids to soccer, did their homework with them; it was great."

In October 2004, Dave was doing heart transplants in Napa, California, for ten days when Karen got a phone call. Dave had been found unresponsive in his apartment. Jess, then seven and in second grade, remembers being ushered home from a sleepover to find their house full of people. Her mom and a pastor met her on the front porch and broke the news.

Dave's family had a history of heart problems, so Karen assumed his death at age thirty-nine was cardiac related. They would have to wait for the autopsy to know for sure.

As the first widow among a growing group of young parents in Salida, Karen felt people staring at her. "I thought getting into a routine was the healthiest thing, so the next Saturday"—six days later—"the kids had soccer, so we went to soccer," she says. "We had to move forward, somehow. I remember people being like, 'Why are you here? This is soccer. Your husband just died.' I'm like, no shit. And I want to throw up right now. But I don't know what else to do. I got dressed today. Yay, me. I really wanted to die. If I didn't have kids, I don't even want to think about it."

Karen Adamson's best friend was a local teacher named Karen Lundberg. At Dave's memorial service, Karen Lundberg collected stories and photos to help Jake and Jess remember their dad. Then she and some of their friends took Karen Adamson to Ojo Caliente Hot Springs, in New Mexico, where they held her in their arms and cried. The Adamsons considered moving back to San Diego to be around Karen's family. "But this town enveloped us," she says. "And I knew, in my heart: nope, this is where we're staying."

Karen Lundberg and her husband, Eric, helped give her a soft nest. He worked as an insurance broker, which enabled his many passions—hang gliding, skiing, backpacking, elk hunting, fly fishing, and mountain biking. He finished the Leadville 100 twice (as did Karen) and helped start Salida's high school mountain bike team. He and Karen took multiple hut trips every winter, sailed across the Atlantic together, and had two children, Garrett and Kelsay. "It was magical—it really was Mayberry," Karen says. "They could walk to school, play in the river, do whatever they wanted."

Then one day Eric found a strange-looking spot on his leg. He suspected the cause was a pesticide that he'd spilled while working in California's almond orchards at age sixteen. He had the cancerous lesion removed, but after a year the illness spread. Doctors took out one of his lungs. He kept hiking thirteen-thousand-foot peaks.

By then, three more Salida parents had died of heart problems or cancer: Dennis "Raggus" Quick, age fifty-seven, in February 2009; Steve Gilmore, forty-eight, in January 2010; and Mary Redfern-White, forty-three, in February 2010. Everyone was intertwined in small-town ways. Eric Lundberg had started to wonder whether Salida was cursed. "It just feels that way because it's a small town," his wife said.

"I grew up in a small town," Eric countered. "This is not normal."

Then his cancer metastasized to his brain. Four months later, on December 26, 2010, he suffered a massive stroke and died. He was fifty-one. Garrett and Kelsay were sixteen and thirteen, respectively. Karen Adamson and her kids picked up the Lundbergs from the hospital and drove them home to Salida, knowing the pain to come, unable to stop it.

—

After Eric's death, people started taking the idea of a curse more seriously. Salida means "exit" in Spanish—was that a sign? "We were like, should we all move?" recalls Karen Lundberg, who had founded and was running a school by then. They pondered who might be next. "It got crazy. *How do we stop this? Do we have control over it?* It's like people who live in towns with fracking. What do you do?"

Everyone leaned on trauma bonds. The girls spent nights at each others' houses, encircling whoever was wounded. Karen Adamson's friends joked that she was the death doula, there to process for others the maelstrom of medical bills and death certificates and funeral receptions since she had been through it first.

For a little more than three years, the curse was dormant. Then, on February 11, 2014, a successful local psychiatrist named Daniel Golin died by suicide. Chuck and Golin had been friends; Golin even called Chuck to meet shortly before he ended his life, but their schedules conflicted.

Chuck's oldest daughter, Faith, realized she had developed a mental checklist for how to handle parent death: Pack for the week, including a sleeping pad if all the beds are taken. Delegate someone to answer the door and receive guests. Deflect the inbound phone onslaught. *I hate that I know how to do this*, she thought.

"It didn't just feel like kids in the community were losing parents," Jess Adamson says. "It felt like all of my immediate friends' parents were dying. And people who stepped in as parent figures after others died, were then dying. The whole thing was bizarre. I just got less and less shocked when it happened."

Golin's death also heightened Faith's fear that her father was next—a premonition that had lingered for years. By then she actually believed everyone in her friend group had to lose a parent. So the following year, when doctors discovered Chuck's heart was enlarged and ordered emergency open-heart surgery on the East Coast, Faith was sure the time had come. "It seemed like my turn," she says, "like he was too good to keep. I mean, we all relied on him so heavily."

Chuck was the first to say there is no point in asking why one person survives and another dies. He, for now, was one of the survivors.

—

Six weeks after her husband's death, Karen Adamson learned the cause. He had died of an accidental drug overdose. This brought more questions than answers. She couldn't bear to tell their children, so she kept the secret for a decade. When people in town asked her what happened, she simply said, "His heart stopped."

She was thirty-seven, terribly lonely, and craved affection in a town that felt like a fishbowl. "I wanted to be held by someone other than one of my best friends' husbands," she says. Nine months after being widowed, she started dating a builder named Eric Bird whom she would marry four years later. She made it clear that Dave was the love of her life, and they never stopped talking about him. Still, her grief remained unresolved. For years she had a dream that Dave returned, only to find her remarried. One of Dave's relatives, when she found out Karen was dating, said, "I cannot believe you would do that to Dave's memory." Karen gradually cared less about what people thought or said. She kept

Dave's photo on her mantel.

When Jess was eighteen, her mom finally told her how her dad had died. "I had him on a pedestal my whole life— this doctor, this high-achieving, amazing social servant, who was unfairly taken from us by the world," Jess says. "So to find out that he was a real human being, with a crazy thing about him that I didn't know, was shocking. But I think we can miss people and know that they were good, and at the same time, it can be true that life is complicated."

Karen Lundberg, meanwhile, didn't start dating until three years after Eric died. Tall and blond with a buoyant smile, she was fifty when her second life began, fraught with many of the same challenges Adamson had faced. Eric was beloved, and some of his friends felt Karen wasn't being "true to him" by seeing someone new. She called them out in person. In 2014, when she remarried, Chuck served as the officiant.

Chuck kept a close eye on all the kids. For a number of reasons, adolescence is considered the worst time to experience grief. It's a phase of life characterized by dramatic change, emotional development, and self-affirmation—all of which scream for parental direction, even if kids push their parents away.

It's estimated that in the United States one in thirteen children will suffer the death of a parent before the age of eighteen. There is limited research on how this impacts adolescents psychologically; most studies depict a pattern of self-destructive behavior that includes substance abuse, promiscuity, and eating disorders. "Because what can I control? I can't control the outside world, but I can control the things I do with my body," says Stacy Smith, a grief counselor and founder of Camp Forget-Me-Not for bereaved children in Colorado. Parents, meanwhile, typically respond in two ways. "They either get hypervigilant, or they peel out."

Chuck knew firsthand what adolescent grief felt like. When he was sixteen, he lost a brother to cancer, but he didn't process it until he became a monk. Terry Joe, his brother, was ten. Their family doctor had misdiagnosed the cancer, allowing it to spread. It became terminal before they knew what it was. Chuck still marvels at how his parents forgave the doctor.

During his dreamwork, Chuck reached a point where he could cry about Terry Joe. He concluded his brother was in heaven, and he had no reason to worry. This freed him to counsel others without projecting his emotional baggage onto them. It also taught him the value of going through trauma instead of around it.

He leaned on this lesson often. Jess Adamson came to him years after her father's death and asked to talk. "I was in a really dark place, the lowest I've felt," she says. Chuck met her in a classroom at Longfellow and listened, then told stories to help normalize her feelings.

He made a point of checking in on Kelsay Lundberg, too, after her father died. She always called Chuck "my second dad." "He just had this guardian presence, over everyone, always," Jess Adamson says.

Sometimes people wondered how the girls survived, propping up the sky as kids. But they didn't just get by. Jess went
on to be valedictorian; others earned full college scholarships.
The trauma of their youth hardened them. It also broadened
their worldview: Even Mayberry wasn't perfect.

9

TRAGEDY/MIRACLE

The Frankensled that Chris Burandt rode into Porcupine Gulch weighed around 680 pounds, including his 150-pound bodyweight, fuel, provisions, and safety gear. Chase Bunting's total weight was around 700. To send such heavy triggers down an avalanche path in deep powder was extremely risky. Burandt, who had five- and seven-year-old children at home, hated daring nature. "If it had been any other situation, I would not have dropped," he says.

X Games gold medal aside, Burandt's comfort and skill in navigating gnarly terrain had made him the face of the sport—a hero to riders around the world. As precarious as the entrance to Porcupine Gulch was, he and Bunting had ridden nastier stuff all the time. Burandt pointed his sled downhill and eased into the descent. Bunting followed. Instead of gunning their engines and hoping for the best, like a runaway train, they tried to stay on top of a snow-covered rock spine that ran vertically toward the bottom. It was so steep that they couldn't control their speed using throttle alone, so they deployed what they call an "elevator," turning their snowmobiles on their side and digging one ski into the snow, relying on friction to slow their drop. If they started to roll, they could rev their throttle to engage the track just enough to propel them forward and keep the nose down.

As the slope tapered, Bunting looked to his left. The entire bowl was moving. An avalanche had fractured higher up, sending a three-foot pile of debris racing downhill. The slide was roughly eighty yards away, closer than the shouts Burandt had heard. There was plenty of snow in it to bury someone; instead, the wave churned past with a low rumble into the forest below. Bunting was used to managing avalanche hazard on the fly, but he still felt a spike of adrenaline. They then continued their descent cautiously. That too triggered a series of small surface sloughs, any of which could have broken deeper and become a lethal slide. The already tense mission took on a more foreboding feel, reminding them to keep moving as quickly as possible.

All the while it continued to snow.

Burandt and Bunting navigated between boulders protruding from the hillside and small trees that had been snapped or bent by past avalanches, their boughs permanently wilted. Finally, Burandt made a beeline onto a natural bench halfway down.

"I start thinking, I am going to yell, and they literally have to be right here," he recalls. "Because that's what it sounded like at the top. I had probably dropped five hundred vertical feet. So, I yell. I get nothing. It really confused me, because this was where the voice was coming from; they should be right here. And I yell, yell, yell—and get nothing. So I keep making my way down and stopping every hundred yards and yelling, and hear nothing." Though he was still in the forest, the trees were widely spaced and the slope had started to relent. A half hour had passed since he'd heard the voice.

Bunting caught up to Burandt at the bottom, which brought momentary relief. At least the steep part was over.

As soon as they got through the trees, they entered a meadow where Burandt saw fresh ski tracks. It had to be Brett and Cole. No one else would have been here in these conditions. Burandt yelled again, to no avail. Theorizing that perhaps Brett and Cole had gotten stuck and then reversed course and tried to go up using the same tracks, he took a left and followed them uphill.

Above and to the west, D-Bone's group heard radio reports relayed from Burandt and Bunting that indicated they had made it to the flats and were hot on the trail. Gab decided to defer to Konigsberg, the state avalanche forecaster, as they proceeded toward Burandt and Bunting's location. Konigsberg led them through the forest as if tiptoeing on his skis so as not to stress the snowpack. He tried to link various safe spots—mini platforms where the slope eased—near sturdier anchors such as thick trees that might hold the slab in place. None felt very safe, however. Audible *whumpf*s and cracks in the snow, clues that often precede avalanches, highlighted the constant danger. "It was nasty, windblown, heavily loaded, fuckin' scary," D-Bone recalls. Hundreds of tons of mass hung on the slope, which loomed above them farther than they could see. He figured if a slab fractured, it might take out the entire forest.

At one point they came across fresh debris—chunks of snow compressed together in a heap—and glanced upward to see a four-foot-tall crown where the avalanche had released. Gab radioed their finding back to the hut. Suddenly everyone wondered whether the slide had buried Brett and Cole. McHargue already had asked neighboring counties to send specially trained dogs that could help locate and recover buried victims. Yet closer inspection revealed no tracks entering or leaving the avalanche, signaling it had occurred naturally. They continued their descent.

As Burandt and Bunting followed the tracks uphill, they noticed two places where it appeared someone had stopped, probably for a while. One was much more established. The snow had been stomped into an eight-foot-wide crater around a tree, with a small bench made of snow in the middle. There was no sign of a fire or more substantial shelter, like a snow cave. *Did they spend the night here?* Burandt shuddered at the thought. It would have made more sense if he'd found something with walls.

Continuing on the tracks, Burandt came to another large meadow—roughly three hundred yards wide, with Porcupine Creek at its edge and an avalanche path above it where prior slides had cleared the vegetation. He scanned the landscape and, less than a football field away, saw a figure lying in the snow. "Brett!" he shouted. "Brett!"

Burandt felt a surge of joy—and relief. He pinned his throttle. *Let's get you out of here!*

As he reached Brett, however, his elation turned to dread. "He was on his back, one ski up in the air, still on his foot," Burandt recalls. "And these are the tough ones, right? This was a look on a man's face that you will never forget. He was still moving and breathing, but he didn't know who I was, or what I was. He kept trying to fight me off."

Burandt was shocked to see how little clothing Brett was wearing: an old blue jacket that had lost its loft, a light base layer underneath, and a pair of worn-out ski pants covered in duct-tape patches—with a tiny day pack that looked more suited to trail running than backcountry skiing. Brett's neck gaiter was hard as wood. His wool hat was frosted. He was wearing the mittens Cole had given him, but his hands were stiff and curled up. One of his legs was locked at the knee, perhaps frozen, perhaps from an injury. Burandt immediately radioed up to his relay near the saddle, a snowmobiler named Brian Wenzel, who then turbo wheeled a couple of hundred yards uphill to share the news with the hut. Burandt told Wenzel that Brett was in bad shape. "We need to get a helicopter right now and fly him out of here." He read off the GPS coordinates. It was a little after 1:30 p.m., twenty-seven hours after Brett and Cole had set off.

There wasn't time yet to think about where Cole might be. Bunting arrived just after Burandt. With snow screaming across the meadow, they gently slid Brett's stiff body up onto Burandt's Frankensled to transport him to where it was calmer near the trees. Brett couldn't extend his arms. He could barely move his head. He groaned a couple of times, but couldn't speak. Burandt drove slowly so as not to jostle Brett. Bunting, meanwhile, raced ahead to the forest. He sawed branches from trees, siphoned gas from his tank, and started a fire. He knew their only hope was to warm Brett up. Once Burandt got Brett to the flames, they replaced his frozen hat, neck gaiter, and mittens with dry ones. They wrapped him in an emergency blanket and bivouac sack, and then Bunting bear hugged him from behind, sitting on the ground facing the fire, to maximize the transfer of warmth. Burandt looked through Brett's pack for anything that might help them. He was stunned to find a bag of uneaten trail mix at the bottom, and water in Brett's canteen. It seemed to them that Brett had exerted himself until he could no longer walk, and then just fallen over.

For a while Brett attempted to get away from them and stand, pushing on Bunting with his arms and bending his good knee to bring his foot under him "He was trying to go do something," Bunting says. "He was very adamant on not just sitting there." Eventually, though, Brett stopped fighting. He entered what Burandt called "a state of calmness and peace." His mouth was open. He couldn't talk, but if Burandt asked a question, he grunted, as if he understood what Burandt was saying.

"Where's the kid?" Burandt asked. "Is the boy okay?"

Brett made a noise that indicated to Burandt he was trying to say something specific. With D-Bone's group getting closer, Burandt turned to Bunting. "Keep the fire going, keep

Brett warm, I'll stay in touch with those guys. I'm going to find the kid."

For the next fifteen minutes Burandt followed the tracks farther up-valley. He saw multiple places where Brett and Cole had tried to ascend, stopped where it got steep, then turned around and circled back to another spot where they tried again. After canvassing all their loops and finding no tracks that continued uphill, Burandt realized Cole had to be below him. He headed down the gulch.

Bunting, meanwhile, kept his arm around Brett at the fire, trying to limit Brett's movement. He knew that hypothermia places a patient's heart in an extremely delicate state, where the slightest stimulation can trigger it to stop beating.

"Brett shook his head a couple times and grunted the word 'no' when I was holding him," Bunting recalls. "It's hard to say why, but he could've been trying to tell me, basically, 'Screw you, man, leave me here and go get Cole.' It was almost like he knew he was done, and that I was wasting my time."

Bunting watched Brett inhale a mouthful of air, then go limp. He immediately laid him down and initiated CPR. Brett's chest cavity rose and fell with each compression. After a minute, to Bunting's amazement, Brett came back. His eyes flickered, his jaw dropped, and he took another breath. Bunting could tell he was fighting as hard as he could to stay alive.

On Burandt's way down the gulch in search of Cole, he left the tracks he was following and returned to check on Bunting and Brett. He arrived just before Brett's heart arrested a second time. Again they resuscitated him. His breathing lasted just a short period, however, before it ceased again.

D-Bone's team was nearing the meadow, breaking trail through thigh-deep snow on their skis, when they heard on the radio that CPR was under way. They knew this meant Brett was in dire shape. Burandt gunned his sled to their location to meet them, picked up Jimmy Dalpes, an EMT, to assist with CPR—as well as a puffer mask that made rescue breaths more efficient—and raced back to Brett. Dalpes checked Brett's femoral and carotid arteries for a pulse, but found none. He knew from working as a raft guide and swiftwater technician that patients with hypothermia can be revived hours after they arrest. But he had to remove Brett from the environment, which at the moment was impossible.

D-Bone already had been brainstorming ways to evacuate Brett—by building a sled with Brett's skis, or strapping him to a snowmobile, perhaps. He knew the ongoing storm almost certainly ruled out a medevac, and without a helicopter, their efforts would take hours. It was now around two o'clock and was only going to get colder and darker. They removed Brett's wet clothes, cocooned him in a pair of sleeping bags, and stuffed small heating packs in his crotch and armpits to warm his core. D-Bone tried sternal rubs— vigorously massaging Brett's sternum with a closed fist, a pain-stimulation technique meant to provoke a response in an unconscious person—to no avail. D-Bone's fingers were nearly numb, but he detected a faint, fluttering pulse (hypothermic subjects often present a very slow heart rate, requiring first responders to check for as long as a minute).

Bump-bump . . . ten-second pause . . . *bump-bump*.

While earning his EMT certification, D-Bone had manually pumped a shooting victim's heart after the man had died. While climbing the Nose on El Capitan in Yosemite National Park, passing the ledge where another climber had fallen without a helmet two days earlier, he'd ascended through human brain matter. But compressing Brett's chest in the middle of nowhere gutted him. This was his kindred spirit. He watched a tear weep out of Brett's eye and start rolling down his cheek. It froze before reaching the bottom.

Back at the hut, Naccarato and McHargue turned down the volume on their radios as updates poured in, trying to protect Brooke. Joel struggled to maintain hope. *How could they have found Brett but not Cole?* Crying at a table, he looked broken, angry. He knew the odds that his son was alive likely decreased if they'd separated. Eventually Naccarato ushered Joel and Chuck outside to talk. Joel was Naccarato's doctor and had delivered his daughter. Naccarato informed them the snowmobilers were following a ski track that they hoped was Cole's. This steadied Joel. He added, "They're working on Brett, but they can't revive him."

"Oh, they'll never be able to, unless they can warm him up," Joel said matter-of-factly. His brain had turned pragmatic even as he feared for his son's life.

Passive rewarming, or applying heat externally, would not be enough to save Brett. He needed active rewarming, or internal heat, a specialized process that usually happens in city hospitals with Level 1 trauma centers.

—

Around this time, Andrew Maddox, a Colorado Parks and Wildlife river ranger and standout snowmobiler whom Burandt had called that morning, began riding toward the mouth of Porcupine Gulch, three miles east. Maddox figured that that entrance was their only hope of evacuating Brett and Cole if they were indeed stuck in Porcupine, because it wasn't as steep as the walls above.

Maddox's sled, a 600cc stock machine, was no match for the conditions he found—what he called "turbo snow." But he pinned his throttle through the flats, over sagging barbed-wire fences that marked private land boundaries, and eventually reached the toe of the gulch.

Built like a rhino at six feet, 220 pounds, with a thick red beard, Maddox was a former all-region defensive end from Nebraska and ski patroller at Monarch. He had been involved in a backcountry miracle before. On March 2, 2013, he was assisting a colleague with a snowmobile fundraiser at State Forest State Park west of Fort Collins. They had just thrown steaks on the grill at the park maintenance shop when a call came through. A large avalanche had been reported on Cameron Pass, twenty miles east. Two people were missing. Maddox and his colleague, Sam McCloskey, loaded up their sleds, jumped in their truck, and rushed to the scene.

They snowmobiled through rugged terrain to reach the

massive debris field, spread out below a quarter-mile-wide fracture line. The crown was six feet tall. Two skiers and a dog had been descending a run called Paradise Bowl when it avalanched. Another party had located and dug up one of the skiers, confirming he was deceased, but despite an extensive search, they couldn't find the second man—a twenty-four-year-old law student named Alex White.

When Maddox and McCloskey had arrived, the mountain was covered in zigzag ski tracks from the prior search. Maddox followed a beacon signal to a spot that didn't appear to have been disturbed. He saw two boot tips poking out of the snow. It looked like they'd wiggled at some point. Assuming this was a body-recovery mission, and with fading afternoon light, he told McCloskey to start digging and then left to find the confirmed fatality, approximately one hundred feet away. By the time he returned, the incident commander had directed them to leave the field. But Maddox knew he wouldn't be able to sleep if he didn't verify for himself that the man was dead. He and McCloskey dug toward White's head, which was much deeper than his boots. It had been more than three hours since the avalanche; someone has a better chance of surviving a head-on collision at seventy miles per hour than lasting that long under the snow. Maddox accidentally jabbed White's leg with his shovel blade. He heard a groan.

"Sam, did you hear that?"

He popped him again. The sound repeated itself. *Oh my God, he's fucking alive*, Maddox thought. They tore into the snow like dogs until they'd uncovered his face.

Soon other rescuers arrived and helped excavate White. They placed him on a snowmobile to be transported back to the trailhead where he would be met by a helicopter. White suffered cardiac arrest during his ride and was resuscitated in the air. His core temperature had dropped to seventy-two degrees—well past the point where most people die. But his outcome served as a reminder to not give up, even when someone is frozen and unconscious. "You're not dead until you're warm and dead," the medical adage goes.

White reached the hospital almost six hours after the avalanche had buried him. Despite two torn knee ligaments and a lacerated calf, he was back at law school within a week. "That guy is alive because two random people who weren't supposed to be there happened to be there that day," Maddox says.

━

Brett already was a candidate for extracorporeal life support, or ECLS, a risky medical procedure that has saved the lives of hypothermic patients around the world. Doctors pump a person's blood out of their body, warm it up, and then pump it back in. The most famous case occurred in May 1999 outside Narvik, Norway. A twenty-nine-year-old radiologist named Anna Bågenholm broke through a frozen creek while backcountry skiing with friends. She became wedged under the ice, submerging her in frigid water. She craned her neck to find an air pocket and continue breathing—until she lost consciousness. An hour and twenty minutes after her fall, rescuers chopped a hole in the ice and pulled her out. She was pulseless, breathless, and white as a bone. By the time a helicopter delivered her to a hospital in Tromsø, her core temperature had plunged to 56.7 degrees—lower than anyone on record had survived. Her heart had stopped beating more than two hours earlier, yet doctors performed ECLS. Later that night, Bågenholm's heart started beating again. The cold had slowed her demise in such a way that it preserved her brain function—a state akin to suspended animation. She regained consciousness after ten days, paralyzed from the neck down; it took years for her to return to her former activities, but she enjoyed an almost complete recovery.

Bågenholm's case became legend in the medical community, and it offered hope for Brett, too.

Images of Brett flickered through Burandt's and Bunting's minds as they plowed through more deep snow, zigzagging around trees like slalom gates, following Cole's track. *If Brett's in that shape, what shape is Cole going to be in? Why weren't they together? If they're not together, is Cole dead?* Burandt didn't know if he could handle seeing a child like that.

Ten minutes down the gulch, Burandt came upon a figure lying in the snow. His heart dropped. It was the same posture he'd seen in Brett, minus the ski sticking up. When he arrived, he saw a boy's face, beet red from twenty-eight hours of exposure—with blinking eyes.

Burandt could tell immediately the kid was in a much better state. He also was more bundled up than Brett, which made them wonder whether Brett had given Cole his clothes.

"Are you the fourteen-year-old who's lost?" Burandt asked, in a moment of astonishment.

"I'm fifteen," Cole snapped. Burandt let slip a grin.

It was 2:17 p.m. Cole had left Brett but traveled just a short distance before stopping once more to wait. By the time help arrived, he had been there for more than an hour.

When Cole asked about Brett, Burandt shook his head. "It seems like he's not going to make it."

Cole sat on a snowmobile and stared at the ground in disbelief.

Burandt and Bunting had brought food for their day, and while Brett had been incapable of eating, Bunting handed Cole his buffalo chicken sandwich, and Burandt gave him his meatball sub. Cole devoured both. He seemed lucid, but something was off. He kept cracking jokes, almost like the seriousness of the situation hadn't hit him. "Man, you wouldn't happen to have an extra Snickers in there, would you?" he deadpanned to Bunting.

Hypothermia is known to trigger various manifestations in one's mental state, from somnolence to irritability to delirium. "It almost seemed like he was in some sort of shock," Bunting says. "Chris and I talked about it, like, we need to get him out of here right now." Despite their concern, however, Cole's extremities were in surprisingly good shape.

When word reached the hut that Cole had been found and that he was talking, Joel and Morgaan broke down and hugged, tears pouring out in tidal surges. Locals in Salida who had been listening to the VHF radio traffic spread the news like Paul Revere. Someone ran into Salida Mountain Sports shouting, "They found Cole! They found Cole!"

Brooke thought of her dad. *Why haven't they said he's okay?* Watching Joel and Morgaan rejoice made her feel more alone.

Burandt and Bunting started another fire, monitoring Cole as his condition improved. When they asked how he and Brett became separated, Cole said Brett told him, "Keep going." So he did. They also asked whether he had heard their earlier shouts from the ridge, and whether he and Brett had yelled back. He said no, which confused them. Only later would Burandt and Bunting learn that they and the rescuers on skis had been shouting to each other, both groups believing they were hearing Brett and Cole.

D-Bone's team took turns performing CPR on Brett for almost two hours. None of them carried tools to make a "burrito wrap," as improvised hypothermia kits are sometimes called. The kits generally include a sleeping bag, a tarp or vapor barrier to seal the outside of the bag, a heat source like hot water in an insulated bottle, and a ground pad that would help preserve whatever warmth a patient still had. Gab sensed Brett was gone, but he knew D-Bone didn't want to give up. So he let their efforts continue for much longer than he would have otherwise. "I can't even describe how cold I was," Gab says. Tiny snowflakes fell like particles of dust.

Finally, Dalpes looked at the other three men. He held the

highest medical standing in the group, and their exposure was weighing on him. Evacuating Brett would require towing him on a sled behind a snowmobile, which they didn't have. Dalpes turned to D-Bone. "I hate to do this," he said, "but we have to leave him. We have to protect ourselves. We'll bring him out tomorrow."

Gab reported a "Code Frank," or fatality in LCSAR's radio parlance—a way to prevent public ears from deciphering the outcome before a victim's family found out.

High on the rim of Porcupine Gulch, Chris Tracy heard they were ceasing CPR and dropped to the snow on his knees, next to his stuck machine. He immediately thought of the time they'd lost that morning. *We just needed one more hour*, he thought. *Give us one fucking hour back.*

D-Bone had been using his backup skis all day, so he swapped them with the ones he'd loaned Brett and stuck his backups in the snow, in an *X*, to mark Brett's location. He removed the sleeping bags in case they needed them later and wrapped Brett in a reflective blanket, red side up for visibility. D-Bone knelt next to his friend, trembling from the cold. He leaned in and kissed Brett on the forehead. Then he began the somber ski out.

They followed Burandt and Bunting's packed snowmobile track for direction and ease of travel. Partway down the drainage, they came across Burandt, Bunting, and Cole. Cole was about to ditch his skis, but D-Bone knew they would come in handy if the machines got stuck, so he strapped them to his pack and kept moving. Bunting rode double with Cole while Burandt navigated ahead of them a path of least resistance. The terrain, pocked with dark, tight timber and a winding creek bed—Gab estimated they jumped the creek on their snowmobiles at least five times in the air—made for a harrowing egress. "What they rode to get out was *insane*," Gab says.

None of the skiers spoke. It felt as if they'd swum a mile out to sea to rescue a drowning friend, only to watch him sink as they reached for his arms.

—

When Joel at the hut learned that Cole was headed to Leadville Junction, he announced, "We're out of here in fifteen minutes." Everyone stuffed what they could into backpacks and prepared to ski back down to the parking lot six miles away. The energy felt spooky, a mix of ecstasy and unease. Brooke remained quiet and withdrawn. It had been more than three hours since they'd found her dad. Neither she nor her mom or sister had received an update on his status. Naccarato couldn't bear to let Brooke descend on her own, so he offered to take her down on his snowmobile. As the rest of the group set off on skis, Brooke wrapped her arms around his trunk, sticking her hands in his pockets, and held on like a koala.

Guilt gnawed at Naccarato the entire way down. He had watched Brooke grow up, seen Brett beam with pride since his daughters were born. Now, he knew from the radio transmissions that Brett was dead—and she didn't.

"Is my dad okay?" Brooke asked.

"Brookie, they're working on him," Naccarato replied. "They're doing everything they can."

"I had to lie to her," he recalls in tears. "And I felt terrible doing it, but I just didn't think it was my place to take that from her."

While Joel's group proceeded to the trailhead, at times flailing in the deep snow, Matt Burkley, Joel's medical partner and Brett's family physician, mounted one final attempt to save Brett. Burkley had delivered Bari and Brooke and been friends with Brett for almost twenty years. He knew how miraculous ECLS could be, having performed the procedure himself. He caught a ride on the back of a snowmobile from Leadville Junction to the cold plain where Porcupine Gulch emptied to the east. There, he met Burandt, Bunting, and Cole on their way out. He hugged Cole, picturing his own son in the same situation, overwhelmed by emotion. "I just had to feel him," Burkley says.

At the very least, Burkley felt he should render an opinion on Brett's state, even if that meant pronouncing him dead. He also secretly wondered whether ECLS might still be possible. Burandt, however, shot that idea down. Entering Porcupine at this hour, with darkness encroaching and in subzero temperatures, was far too risky. Burkley protested, but others backed Burandt's assessment and eventually Burkley conceded.

In Salida, Cari and Bari knew that Brett had been found, but his condition remained unclear. Bari hoped any damage would be superficial. *Maybe he'll lose some toes and fingers*

*from frostbite, or part of his nose. I don't care if he looks dif-
ferent. He'll still be my dad.*

One of Cari's friends volunteered to drive them to Leadville, assuming Brett would be taken to St. Vincent hospital.
For a few minutes their house turned into a circus. Cari frantically gathered clothes for Brett. Her friends talked to their
husbands at the parking lot, asking for updates. Suddenly
Bari noticed people weren't packing as urgently anymore.
One of Cari's friends said, "Slow down. Let's just wait until
we hear more." And immediately, Cari knew. A text came
through. "I'm so sorry," it read. Cari started pacing, waiting
for an official declaration—for life as she knew it to end.

The vehicles at Leadville Junction were buried by fresh snow
when Naccarato pulled into the parking lot with Brooke
nearing five o'clock. He escorted her to an idling LCSAR
truck, where someone held the door for her. "I felt like the
pied piper," he says. "It was one of the hardest things I've
ever done." Anita Mason made sure the SAR radio was off.

About twenty minutes later, Bunting rode up on his
snowmobile carrying Cole. What should have been cause for
celebration—a missing boy being returned alive—instead
was marked by who wasn't there. To those who already
knew, Cole's appearance magnified an unbearable, unthink-
able truth. Brett Beasley was gone.

Mason didn't get much time with Cole in the parking lot,

but she asked the same question Burandt had asked in Porcupine Gulch: How did he and Brett get separated? Cole told her what he had told them: Brett had instructed him to keep going. So he did.

Soon Chuck, Joel, Morgaan, and Melissa arrived, having been picked up on Turquoise Lake Road by a Forest Service worker driving an all-terrain vehicle. Joel and Morgaan rushed over to Cole, and the three of them embraced in the dark. Morgaan heard every inch of Cole's frozen red jacket crunch when she hugged him. "We're so glad you're okay," Joel wept to his son. "We love you so much."

Once more the Schalers' relief cut Brooke like a blade. For two days she had felt a kinship with Joel and Morgaan— they were all in a similar state, frantic and vulnerable, trying to maintain hope. Morgaan had served as something of a big sister to Brooke, holding her close at hard moments. Now, suddenly, Brooke was on her own.

Melissa climbed into the back seat of Mason's truck to be with Brooke. LCSAR members came and went, aware that Brett was dead yet trying to shield Brooke until they received permission from the sheriff or coroner to inform his family. Finally Mason talked to Sheriff Fenske. She figured it would be best if Jason Horning, a pastor and LCSAR member who had spent much of the day at the hut, broke the news to Brooke.

Horning, a rock climber from Detroit and father of three, had officiated funerals for children killed in car wrecks, delivered last rites to strangers, and comforted families as loved ones took their last breath. But rarely had he done so for a parent in the prime of his life, as Brett was, and almost never after a sudden event. He knew the latter scenario brought more confusion, fear, and anger than when people had a chance to prepare.

As Horning approached Mason's truck, Brooke saw him coming and knew. He opened the rear passenger door, where she sat. "I'm really, really sorry, Brooke. We tried CPR, we did everything we could." He never said Brett was dead, but he didn't have to. Brooke crawled over Melissa, away from Horning, threw open the door, and sprinted toward a snowbank a hundred feet away. A piercing scream exploded from her chest, echoing across the valley. Anyone who was there still chokes up recalling the sound. Brooke writhed in the snow, sobbing and screaming.

Melissa stood in the parking lot searching for her father to comfort her, bawling like a lost child.

Horning walked over to Brooke and prayed aloud. "Lord, please let her know she's not alone. Please be present."

Two dozen burly, dazed men—the men who had searched for Brett and yearned to do more to save him—watched from the fringe, wincing at the sight and sound of a daughter mourning her father. Horning called Cari and told her Brett was dead, confirming the stabbing sensation she already felt in her heart. Cari then told Bari, who ran to the bathroom, locked the door, and collapsed onto the floor, wailing.

Longtime Salida resident Loni Walton, an old friend of Brett's, had stood outside all day in the parking lot to share in his suffering. Now she collected his daughter from the snowbank, wrapping Brooke in her arms. Walton started her truck and helped Brooke inside, still distraught. Brooke called Cari. "My dad's dead," she cried, aching to be back in Salida.

Brooke immediately blamed herself. "He didn't even want to come," she sobbed to Walton. "Today's his birthday, and he didn't even want to come on this trip."

Walton, like most Salidans, was dumbfounded by the turn of events. How could rescuers have found Brett alive, only to see him die in their care?

Brooke couldn't help but feel as if Cole's family had won and hers had lost. She walked toward the Schalers full of questions. *What were my dad's last hours like? His last words? What* happened?

"I want to talk to Cole," Brooke said, expecting his input would help her understand. She and Cole climbed into Walton's warm truck. Everyone else, including Walton, stood outside and waited.

"What did he say to you?" Brooke asked.

Cole didn't know how to respond. "He just kept saying how much he loved you guys."

Cole explained that he and Brett had shared a granola bar the night before, and that they had cuddled in the crater to stay warm. He described being rescued by Burandt and Bunting. "They gave me a sandwich, and it was, like, the best sandwich I've ever had in my life."

Brooke burned inside. *How dare you say that to me. My dad can't eat a sandwich.*

Shortly after they'd gotten into the truck, Brooke opened

the door and got out, appearing shaken. Cole exited the other side. Neither told anyone else what was said.

Cole struggled to comprehend what had happened. For thirty hours he'd been despondent; now he was ecstatic; but, someone had just died. He had to answer questions and go to the hospital; on Monday, he had school.

Moments after Brooke and Cole's conversation, the Schalers loaded into Joel's truck and left for St. Vincent in Leadville. During the drive, Cole seemed lucid. But when they entered the emergency room, his demeanor changed. He couldn't provide straightforward answers. He made random statements to the nurses and doctors, then laughed. "Something wasn't right," Morgaan recalls. "Cole was never upset, never crying, just kind of joking around like *nothing* had happened."

"Are you okay?" she asked him. "You don't seem okay."

Whether his behavior was coherent or a subconscious defense mechanism, Cole's health was surprisingly fine. He complained of numbness in his toes and fingers—a lingering effect of the long snowmobile ride out—and his temperature was a couple of degrees lower than normal. Joel and Morgaan mostly refrained from probing about his ordeal, save for one question.

"Did you feel Mom out there?" Morgaan asked.

"I've never felt closer to her," Cole replied.

—

Cari had requested that Chuck drive Brooke home in their

4Runner with Mike Potts. Brooke and Melissa sat in the back, holding hands. Potts barely said a word. Brooke saw how lifeless and sad her dad's best friend looked; she figured he was a reflection of her own appearance.

Finally, she could no longer hold in her heartbreak. "Chuck," she blurted out, "I'm only fifteen! I don't know what to do!"

Chuck pulled over and put the car in park. He turned to face Brooke. "I know you don't know what to do," he said. His mind flashed back to other girls who had lost parents. "Here's how this works. We're going to pull up to your house, and there's going to be people there. And they love you and they're well intentioned, and the hard part is they want to comfort you but at the same time hear that you're okay. And you're not okay right now, Brooke." He paused. "You just walk in that door, and you don't owe anything to anybody. Grab your mom or sister and say, 'I need to be with you.' That'll give you space to land, and they can help you from there. But you don't have to give hugs to everybody who wants to give you hugs. And you're right, Brooke. You're fifteen. And nobody knows how to do this."

Chuck restarted the car and drove to Salida. When he pulled up to the Beasleys' house, Cari came out and ushered her daughter inside. She and Bari and Brooke embraced, like the Schalers had done two hours earlier—clinging to what remained of their family. Brooke collapsed. Someone removed her boots. Cari and her daughters sat together in disbelief.

That night, Brett's friends wandered around Salida's

empty, snow-covered streets struggling to breathe. Brooke checked her phone and saw she had three hundred new follow requests on Instagram, a sign of the spotlight to come.

Some seventy miles north, in the depths of the Sawatch Range, Brett lay surrounded by the natural splendor he had always sought. The storm had ended; the sky had cleared. An ocean of stars sparkled above him.

PART 3
THE RECKONING

What matters is not how long you live but how well; and
often living well means that you cannot live long.

–Seneca, Epistles 101.15

10

EVEN RAINBOWS END

S alidans woke up to a rare sight the next morning: deep snow blanketing the valley from the river to the peaks. Usually storms only dusted the town, even when they caked the skyline. Mike Reed, one of Brett's oldest friends—a rural Kansas boy who had followed Brett to Salida from K-State, had lived in Brett's garage, and had taken a Forest Service job that Brett had lined up—felt he had to go skiing. It was tugging at him, the blue sky and fresh powder. The famous mohawked skier Glen Plake once said that after something went wrong in his life, only skiing could make it right. Reed had come home from the search feeling like he'd been sledgehammered in the forehead. His ten-year-old daughter's words echoed in his mind during the drive up Monarch Pass. "He died on his birthday, Daddy. He made it full."

In the parking lot, Reed bumped into Nate Porter, also

skiing solo. Porter owned Salida's outdoor shop and had been friends with Brett since they met in a Wilderness First Responder (WIFR) course in the late '90s. Brett took the class for work. Porter took it because he'd survived an avalanche that killed his friend, and he wanted to become better prepared for when nature turned. In that accident, in late April 1995, Porter and three buddies triggered a massive slab on the east face of 14,115-foot Pikes Peak above Colorado Springs, where they lived. The slide engulfed Porter and washed him over an eighty-foot cliff. He landed on his knees, somehow spared from serious injury, and went searching for his partners. One had a broken femur, another a broken hip. He found Bill Blair, a father of five, dying from a head wound. The event forever changed Porter's view of the mountains, but not his need for them. He still skied five days a week if the snow was good.

Reed and Porter skinned up to the ridge, reflecting on what they knew and what they didn't. For a long time, they hugged. Then they skied. The levitation was transfixing, like a mute button to the rest of life's noise. At the bottom Reed collapsed onto his back. The sparkling crystals enveloped him, and for a moment, staring at the cerulean sky, all he felt was peace.

Under different circumstances, they would have done whatever they could to ski all day. But after two runs, they returned to the parking lot, cracked a beer, and cranked the Grateful Dead. Reed relied on the Dead's lyrics to express what he was feeling. Songs like "Saint of Circumstance"— *Well it's been heaven, but even rainbows end*—and "He's

Gone" comforted him.

"That day reinforced why I love doing it, with the people I love doing it with, and why I love living here," Porter says. He had done the same after his 1995 accident: As soon as his physical wounds healed, he returned to Pikes Peak and skied. "There's something about backcountry skiing, powder skiing, that in the face of tragedy—as counterintuitive as it may seem to the layperson—that's pretty much the only way I could think of to act. We certainly weren't going to be able to start finding solace or understanding by sitting around our house wondering what happened."

On the other end of the Sawatch that morning, Burandt, Bunting, and Maddox snowmobiled in to retrieve Brett's body. Some of his friends, including Naccarato and Trail, waited at the mouth of Porcupine Gulch. Bunting towed Brett wrapped on a makeshift gurney to where his friends stood, then got off his machine while they said goodbye. Naccarato sat next to Brett with his hand on Brett's chest, feeling him one final time. They rode in a procession back to the trailhead, like an honor guard, three sleds on either side. McHargue thanked Burandt for all that he and Bunting had done. "It's not normal that we need such good resources, but if we need it again, can we call you?" McHargue asked. Burandt said sure.

LCSAR held an impromptu debrief—what they call a hot-wash—at their cache in Leadville. Members tried to make sense of a mission that had overwhelmed their team and left them questioning its cause. "We pull so many people off of Elbert and Massive who have no clue," Horning, the pastor, says. "They're up there in denim and cotton with a little water bottle and a couple granola bars and think they're okay. But it's another thing to have a local who knows better—that's what it felt like. All he needed was a couple of things." Like a cell phone, a map, warmer clothes, a fire starter. Still, enough backcountry rescuers have themselves needed help over the years that they try not to judge their subjects.

Potts had driven up to collect a trinket from Brett, anything that he might take with him as a reminder of his friend's spirit. When he saw that Brett already had been packaged, he sat in the parking lot with a pen and paper. He thought about their old friend Lance Hassler, who'd been a lone survivor like Cole now was. After Lance died, at age thirty-four, Brett had gone back to Kansas to speak at his funeral. Moved by the experience, he had told Potts, "Whichever of us dies first, the other has to say something about him." So Potts wrote a speech right there in his truck. Among his lines:

He loved this valley and did all he could to make it a better place to live and visit.

I don't know if you could have a better friend than Brett.

Cari was his greatest passion of all.

That night, D-Bone walked down the alley that he and Brett shared to Brett's garage, grabbed a bottle of cheap whiskey from the shelf, and tipped it to the ceiling. The Grateful Dead YouTube channel they'd been watching before Brett left for the hut was still playing on the TV. D-Bone belted out Jerry's lyrics as loudly as he could, releasing an emotional waterfall. "God dammit, dude," he said to Brett.

"Why the fuck. You? Really?"

Soon after, D-Bone quit his dream job as a hutmaster and stopped skiing. Other friends of Brett couldn't even *look* at mountains for weeks.

At the Schalers' house on January 6, Cole sat on his couch with a blanket and heating pad on his lap. He and his best friend, Jesse Burns, who'd come over to cook breakfast, stared at the television in silence, watching cartoons. Morgaan walked past and grabbed Cole's hand for a dance, giddy, still celebrating his survival. An acquaintance dropped by with a jug of soup and found Joel outside shoveling snow. Joel immediately launched into the story from start to finish, unblinking, still raw.

Disbelief permeated the community. No one knew how to rationalize what had happened or where to get answers. Potts drove to a friend's condo at Copper Mountain, ninety minutes north, and skied for two days, alone. On his way home, just south of Leadville, a movement caught his peripheral vision. He turned to see an enormous bull elk running toward the highway—the biggest he'd ever seen. He watched it push through deep snow like a plow blade, tossing powder over its head and antlers, a majestic show of natural ferocity. He thought only one thing.

Beasley.

━

Morgaan was asleep when she awoke to Cole's voice from across the hallway. "No, no, I can't go," he said. He had experienced night terrors since he was young, but this seemed different—less random. It was the night after his rescue. She walked into his bedroom and tried to comfort her brother. "Cole, you're okay. You're okay," she said.

"I can't go," he repeated. "You can't let them take me."

"Who?" Morgaan asked.

"No, I have to stay," he continued, panting. Eventually he calmed down, but the next night it happened again. He never woke up or remembered. Morgaan couldn't help but think the episodes stemmed from Porcupine Gulch.

On Monday, four days after he rode out on Bunting's snowmobile, Cole went back to school. He hoped to slide in quietly. But as soon as he parked his bike and walked in the door, friends came over and hugged him. Sitting in class felt awkward, like he was being observed.

Bari and Brooke stayed away. For ten days they and Cari slept on a mattress in their living room. Each morning they got up and hammered through a workout of burpees and pushups, then put the bed away to receive guests. Friends brought food, but they couldn't eat. They spent much of their time telling stories, looking at photos, laughing and crying at once. They avoided discussing what actually happened in Porcupine Gulch, mostly because they didn't know.

Bari was afraid to go on a run, lest anyone see her. She had no idea what she wanted people to say, or how to act herself. One of Brooke's friends wrote her a song about cold and skiing and death, which only elevated her pain. Later, another friend's dad, who she knew was uber religious, told her not to worry about losing her "earthly father" because she still had her "heavenly father." It felt like a smack in the face. She woke in the night hyperventilating; Cari and Bari calmed her down. She had no capacity to do anything, except cry and stare into space. She wasn't interested in seeing her peers, whose visits felt forced. She liked talking only to adults who'd known Brett and had lost something too. When Bari finally reengaged socially, playing pool volleyball with friends at the Salida Hot Springs pool—the same pool where her high-school team had practiced the day he went missing—not one mentioned her dad's death.

Karen Lundberg, who had taught Bari in school, brought Cari journals. "Write everything down," she said, "because as time goes on you will forget."

Karen Adamson dropped off a bag of bagels and a book called *I'm Grieving as Fast as I Can: How Young Widows and Widowers Can Cope and Heal* that had helped her when Dave died. "Just be prepared," she told Bari when she answered the door. "People say some stupid things." Cari's friends came by every day, sometimes toting their toddlers, intent on not isolating her. They agonized over their words but became a shield of sorts from the celebrity of tragedy, opening a fund for the girls and collecting money from those who insisted on giving.

On January 9, LCSAR hosted an incident debrief in Leadville. Team leader Mike McHargue, who ran the mission at the hut, presented a clinical recap of what happened, along with a timeline. Often in a fatal accident, a series of small mistakes creates a much bigger tragedy. This is known as the Swiss cheese model—"when all the holes line up"—and it was especially true in Brett's case. His and Cole's lack of communication, disorientation, and inadequate gear and clothing were exacerbated by a once-in-a-decade storm, which happened to hit their exact area harder than anywhere else (weather stations six to eight miles from Uncle Bud's recorded a third of the snowfall that searchers reported at the hut).

Someone at the meeting suggested that Joel—the only member of their party to attend the debrief—should have known the storm would be worse than the four-inch forecast he'd seen, which stung. The message seemed to be that if they had been aware of how gnarly the conditions would get, they would have proceeded more cautiously and in unison from the hut. McHargue included a slide that detailed the NOAA weather report from the evening Brett and Cole spent in Porcupine Gulch. "Total accumulations one to two feet with locally higher amounts possible," it read. "Snow rates: 1 to 2 inch per hour rates today and Thursday . . . wind gusts to 50 mph through Thursday . . . white out conditions are expected."

D-Bone also attended. He questioned why LCSAR didn't seem adequately prepared to deal with hypothermia—and its lack of urgency when time clearly mattered. "It created a tense scene.

Soon after the debrief, the Schalers went over to the Beasleys' house for a brief, spontaneous visit while others were there too. Everyone's wounds were still dripping, but they wanted to show their support. "Brett saved my life," Cole said to Cari. Joel recalls: "We were just trying to break down some of the barrier, to remember that we're all human beings and we can support each other, rather than just going to our corners and never speaking again. It seemed like we needed to face the beast."

A week or so later, the Schalers invited Cari, Bari, and Brooke to their house on Blake Street to make pizza. The Beasleys sat across from Cole in the living room. He had tried to delay the meeting, afraid of facing Brett's family for a longer duration. Did they think it was his fault that Brett had died? Were Brooke and Bari angry he hadn't saved their dad? He knew from losing his mother that no words could ease their pain. The whole situation felt out of his control, just like it had in Porcupine Gulch.

Everyone hoped to learn more about what happened— how did it get so dire so quickly? Brooke mostly kept to herself while Cari and Bari, as well as Morgaan and Joel, asked questions, careful to keep the conversation light. Cole gave just a broad overview, that they were lost and cold and spent the night in a makeshift shelter. Morgaan was determined to protect her brother from too much probing. After awhile, Bari looked at Cole and cleared the air. "We're really grateful you survived," she said. "Our dad couldn't have lived with himself if the roles were reversed."

Morgaan tried to offer perspective from losing her mother. "I found when you lose a parent, no one can relate to you unless they've been there. So if you ever need somebody to talk to, we're here."

For a bit, they did convene. Morgaan got coffee a few times with Brooke before she went back to college, but eventually their communication stopped. Morgaan assumed it was because her family became a trigger for Brooke.

—

Brett's death made headlines for weeks in Salida's daily newspaper, the *Mountain Mail*. He had been such a leader in town. He used to hike up every fall, even in a driving rainstorm, and string Christmas lights around the giant *S* on Tenderfoot Mountain; one story chronicled how Potts and others rearranged the lights into a *B* after he died. "I think it's appropriate for Brett Beasley's light to shine over the valley for a few more days," Potts was quoted as saying. In the same edition, Chad Hixon, who'd helped found an off-road motorcycle club with Brett's encouragement, said, "The work he did will affect generations."

The next day, January 11, the paper published a half-page account of the "last days of Brett Beasley's life," submitted by Joel. In it he wrote that Brett and Cole "built a snow cave" and spent the night in it. Though a matter of semantics—using "snow cave" instead of "crater"—it created a storyline in people's minds that differed from reality. The piece went on: "In the morning (Jan. 5) they decided to try to ski down and out Porcupine Gulch. However, Brett was unable to warm up and at some point he began to fall a lot"—a detail that Cole had shared with his father—"finally not being able to continue. Cole went on for help." When rescuers found Brett, he "pointed in the direction Cole had gone"—something that Burandt had told Joel and Naccarato, despite having discovered Brett incoherent. "It's clear his priority was to save Cole's life." Joel later submitted a letter to the editor thanking those who supported his family and the Beasleys. "We are so sad to have lost such a good man, father, husband and friend in Brett," the letter read. "He will be greatly missed."

A couple of regional papers covered Brett's death, and one day Bari decided to read the comments online. People skewered Brett for backcountry skiing when he had children, for backcountry skiing in a storm, for taking a child into the wild, for being unprepared. Bari was devastated. It felt as if they had attacked her father *and* her lifestyle.

Despite Salida's history of parent death, Brooke and Bari were the first in their friend groups to lose one. Brooke felt jealous of her peers. Chuck warned Melissa she would become a reminder of the hut trip and to not take it personally if Brooke pulled away from her—which happened immediately. Melissa had been traumatized, too, but the notion of "being okay" had changed. *Brooke isn't okay. Cole isn't okay. I'm fine*, she thought. She couldn't stop feeling guilty for having invited Brooke, which was why Brett had come, which was why Brooke no longer had a dad.

Brooke, meanwhile, felt like everyone was staring at her all the time. To meet their expectations she either had to appear completely fine or on the verge of a breakdown. She chose the former. Cole did the same. It was hard enough for him to see Brooke and Bari in the school halls, but because Cari was the school nurse, he often crossed her path too. He wondered what to do. Say hi every time he saw her? Once in a while? Walk by in silence like he always had? The last thing he wanted was to be unsympathetic, but he had no idea how to express his sorrow, or whether they wanted to hear it from him at all.

The accident became taboo at school, something students whispered about only on weekends. But as the Winterfest dance approached, it took center stage again. Brooke and Cole hadn't relinquished their crushes on each other, despite the fallout from Uncle Bud's. When word spread that they were going together to one of the biggest events on Salida's teenage calendar, people assumed everything must be back to normal. The dance was on February 5, one month after Brett's death. Brooke still steamed from Cole's sandwich comment, but she was also grateful he was alive and, in a strange way, felt the event had made him a bigger part of her life. So although she told friends she wanted nothing to do with him, her need for validation left her seeking his affection as much as, if not more than, she had before the trip. *This brings me closer to him*, she thought. She ached for Cole to tell her more about her dad's last conversations, to say he was sorry for her pain—anything. But neither brought it up that night of the dance.

Five days later, hundreds of people filed into the high school gymnasium for Brett's memorial service. The crowd overflowed into hallways; many sat on the floor. Brooke sang "Beautiful Things" by Gungor. Cole watched from the back, baking under the glare of an imagined spotlight. Everyone else knew Brett as an idol, and all he got to see was a dying dad in his most desperate moment. Did these people blame him for their hero's death? Why couldn't he stop thinking it was his fault?

An autopsy had revealed Brett's heart was enlarged, which fit the legend. (It was impossible to know, however, whether this was biological or due to the cold.) Potts spoke. So did Ben Lara. "He taught us that when you roll up your sleeves and sweat next to someone who appears to have differing views, inevitably common values toward the natural environment emerge," Lara said. He added: "In some ways I don't think we could handle the loss of someone like Brett if it weren't for the community he created. . . . We have a deep sense of gratitude toward the Beasley family as we appreciate the sacrifice you all have made in sharing Brett with us."

Bari chose to speak too. Brett had taken her to a number of funerals, and he often got up to talk about the deceased even if he didn't know them well. He told her it was an important thing to do. So she faced her fear and lightened the mood by recounting his whimsical dream—selling the house and living in his VW bus wherever she went to college, hawking candles that he'd made. Everyone, including Bari, understood he just didn't want to let her go.

After the speeches, one of Cari's friends encouraged her to talk to Chris Burandt, even though she didn't want to. Burandt told her about how Brett had pointed to where Cole was, and how once Brett knew Cole would be rescued, he seemed to let go, as if his job were done. Cari felt better hearing that. Burandt knew Brett hadn't actually pointed in the literal sense, but he justified the story based on his assumption of Brett's intent when he had grunted and lifted his arm.

Burandt also ran into Joel, who thanked him again for saving his son. They got to talking, and Joel described his decision not to follow Brett and Cole's ski tracks into Porcupine Gulch. Burandt suddenly couldn't speak. It was the first time he had heard that someone knew where they'd gone. He thought about the hours he spent waiting at the trailhead and searching blindly around the hut. "If I'd had that information, I would've pulled up there, followed their tracks down, and found Brett at ten o'clock when he was still able," Burandt says, "instead of one o'clock when he was done." He opted not to say as much to Joel, since it was too late to change the outcome. But his shock highlighted a glaring failure in the search: poor coordination between the government and civilian teams.

Burandt wasn't alone in his anger. Chris Tracy, who had alerted the masses with his Instagram post, still regrets waiting at the parking lot under LCSAR's orders. "I don't know why we fucking listened, for as long as we did," he says. "Why did we question who we were and what we were there for—what needed to be done?" His eyes welled up with tears. "It's like, if you're gonna hold us back and not release us, and then you're gonna release us but not give us the point last seen or a radio, then it becomes a geocache game where it's like, who's gonna win? It's your team against our team now, and that doesn't make any sense, because we're trying to accomplish the same thing."

Salidans wrestled with the fact that Brett had died doing something relatively basic. But that wasn't part of the memorial service; it couldn't be. Instead, people sought only to celebrate what made him special.

Brett's after-party happened at A Church, the last place many had seen him alive. His music partners took turns at an open mic. His friends sold T-shirts and posters and stickers ("The man. The Myth. The Legend"), handing Cari wads of cash at the end of the night. The event offered a semblance of closure to those who had been waiting for it—but no clarity about what happened. There were whispers, questions—*What have you heard?* Everyone knew the key to the mystery belonged to one person, and he wasn't at the party.

Perhaps the most complicating factor in the accident's aftermath started with a dog walk. Joel was wired and confused, unsure what his role should be yet unable to wind down. Part of him wanted to get to know Brett so he could better understand who had taken his son on that hasty outing, and who ultimately helped keep him alive. He also felt strangely protective of Cari, having just been widowed himself, and compelled to offer solace and support.

So they went on a walk. And another. Then a hike up S Mountain. Initially it helped them both to process the event. Cari described some of Brett's challenging traits, saying that trying to rein in his energy was like having a third child. She remained uneasy, especially when they hiked past a spot where she and Brett had worked on the trail. But Joel filled her in about the hut trip, which no one had done. She told him she was the kind of person who might not reach out on her own. He thought she needed distractions. One night some of his friends were going out to dinner, so he invited her and picked up their tab. Later, he took her to a concert in Crested Butte. "There was some attraction there," he admits.

Cari, however, wasn't ready to receive any romantic overtures, from Joel or anyone else. At least not yet. She had been with Brett for twenty-six years, and after a while Joel's calls and texts only highlighted how much she missed her husband. His efforts also raised eyebrows among Brett's friends, who were in mama-grizzly mode when it came to Cari and her girls. The whole situation seemed ironic: Cole couldn't open up to the Beasleys about what had happened, and his dad was almost too available. Eventually Cari stopped replying.

11

HOLLOW GAINS

In the months after the hut trip, Joel desperately sought a way into his son's mind. Cole was barely out of eighth grade when Laurie died, and now he was fully immersed in high school, a more vulnerable position. The glare concerned Joel, as did the mystery. "I would love to talk about this if you feel comfortable," Joel often said, unaware that his son already thought about it so much that the idea of more stressed him out.

It wasn't that Cole never spoke of his ordeal. It was that he didn't venture beneath the surface, where the trauma lurked. "I've never been so cold in my life," he told friends who asked about it, hoping they wouldn't pry. And he certainly didn't want to hear how others felt about it. After running through the basic details for his father once, soon after his rescue and mostly to appease Joel, he deflected all future inquiries.

The Schalers may have "won" by getting Cole back, but they were far from whole or happy. Cole was essentially still trying to survive, only in a different milieu. Escaping physical danger had been just part of his escape. Now there was the emotional torture to navigate. Focusing on himself, as his mother always encouraged, seemed the only way to do it. He walked around school wearing earbuds and took up cooking to cope.

After his freshman year ended, Cole and his buddy Jesse—who had stayed up all night praying while Cole was missing—left for Europe. They spent two and a half months on their own, anchored by a soccer residency in Germany. Suddenly Cole wasn't thinking about the hut trip, or his mother's death. Like his father had done when he was a teenager, he grew from experience, traveling by rail, drinking with friends, cliff jumping into the ocean. One night they got on the wrong train and ended up stranded in a sketchy industrial area, out of money and afraid. While waiting to hop the next train, they watched a windowless van pull up to a bridge, snatch someone from the underpass, and speed off. It was terrifying but the ordeal built a measure of resolve in their sixteen-year-old brains. "If we can make it through that," Cole told Jesse later, "and be lost in a country where we don't speak the language, and watch someone get thrown in a van under a bridge, we're good."

In September 2017, while shaving, Joel noticed the left side of his neck appeared thicker than the right. Perplexed, he visited a specialist, who biopsied his lymph node. The result stunned them: Joel had Stage 4 non-Hodgkin's lymphoma throughout much of his body. He couldn't remove it or cure it; treatment was his only hope for remission. Research supported trying immunotherapy, which shrank the tumor; but after a while it grew again, pushing his trachea to the side. He needed chemotherapy.

Joel quietly wondered whether the lymphoma explained the fatigue he'd felt at the hut, when he had opted not to join the search with D-Bone. His kids, meanwhile, reeled from another blow—cancer diagnoses in both parents in less than fewer than twenty months. Still, Joel's prognosis didn't seem as dire as Laurie's, which had struck like utter doom. His chance of survival was substantially better, and he was committed to trying whatever remedy was available.

In November 2017, Joel's life turned again. One of Laurie's longtime acupuncture patients, who had led a weekly meditation group in Laurie's office for seven years, started joining Joel for walks. Tracey Thiele was tall and blond and lived at an old dairy farm on the river. Joel was Tracey's doctor, but they'd never had a real conversation. Over time, she would become his partner and sounding board.

Instead of a hut trip that winter, Joel took Morgaan and Cole to Belize—the intention being to avoid the backcountry, while still bonding in nature. They joined a guided river tour almost one year to the day after Brett's death. A freak accident occurred near the end of the tour: A tourist fell out of his kayak and got trapped in a small, recirculating wave. By the time they pulled him out, he was unconscious and without a detectable pulse. Joel performed mouth-to-mouth resuscitation while someone else delivered chest compressions. Locals rushed him to the hospital, where he survived. Morgaan and Cole became convinced their family was cursed.

Morgaan had transferred colleges by then, leaving Grand Junction to attend the University of Colorado at Colorado Springs. She wanted to be closer to Cole. She attended his soccer games that fall and generally tried to assume the role her mother had once filled. In older stages of loss, like at Morgaan's age, experts have theorized that losing a parent can cause "child parentification," essentially spurring a son or daughter to become a surrogate, which in turn threatens their independence and natural separation from the surviving parent. Morgaan used a range of tactics to cope, enrolling in safety and survival courses, learning to build snow caves and tie ropes, and preparing for all kinds of desperate scenarios. But the added role she took on as it related to Cole—and, eventually, her father when he was diagnosed with lymphoma—also prevented her from addressing her own need to heal.

Alone in Colorado Springs, Morgaan fell into what her father called "a dark place." Anger lingered from her mother's death—the anger that Laurie had let her fear of Western medicine block her from getting early care and then led her to decline treatment. Morgaan couldn't bear to be alone with her thoughts. "Most of the time," she says, "I just felt like I was surviving. I remember this point of crying on my bathroom floor. I've never contemplated suicide, but I had thoughts of not wanting to be here anymore."

It took years of therapy, but she eventually came to terms

with her mother's death. "I just realized that was her decision to make, and maybe that was the wrong one, and maybe
she knew that in the end and she had to live with that," she
says. "And that's really, really hard."

Joel, meanwhile, remained trapped in his own mental
swamp. When he had been a professional guide, he and his
colleagues had debriefed every trip in depth: what went
right, what went wrong, how to be safer the next time. Now
all he could do was recount the hut trip to friends—or, ab-
sent a listener, replay the details in his mind, over and over,
like a GIF. He woke up thinking about it, rehashed it in the
shower, at work, in his living room, on the trail. At the end
of a long day seeing patients, when his colleague Matt Burkley popped into Joel's office and asked, "How ya doing?,"
Joel often launched into the story and didn't stop until it
was over. Tracey heard it dozens of times. So did Chuck.

At one point Joel told it to a female friend whom he'd
guided with at Outward Bound. "It sounds like he put Cole
at risk," she said of Brett.

"Yes," Joel replied, "he did."

He alternated between sadness and rage, grappling with
his conflict as if trying to tame an alligator. "You know, I
grieve for Brett, but as an adult, why didn't you tell me you
were taking off with my son? Because I'm here to spend time
with my kids; that's the whole idea," Joel says, reflecting
on the tumult. "I think Brett was a very competent person,
but any of the people I've done outdoor stuff with would
say, 'Okay, this is our plan, let's stick together.' You don't
just grab somebody's kid and go." He paused. "But I'm also

thankful, because I'm sure Brett felt this awesome responsibility to ensure that Cole survived. And he paid with his life."

Joel didn't ignore his own role in what happened, either. He was Cole's protector and had missed their departure. It happened fast, yes, but he too could have communicated better. Why hadn't he kept a closer eye on Cole that morning? How could he have let him slip away, when the whole point was to be together? This analysis stung the most. He tested Cole's skins on Monarch Pass weeks later, needing to see for himself that the glue was weak. He kept hoping to uncover a clue that would somehow explain what had gone wrong. His quest only perpetuated his suffering.

Joel wanted to share with Bari and Brooke what Brett had told him at the hut, about how much he loved them and yearned to be closer to them. Kids who lose a parent should hear those things, he believed. One day he bumped into Bari at Heart of the Rockies Regional Medical Center in Salida. They shared a friendly exchange. "If you want to get together sometime and have a cup of tea, I'd love to hear what you're doing," Joel offered. Bari said she would be open to that and listed what days she was usually in town. But they never made it happen.

—

In addition to Cole's public silence, the lack of an official accident report, as there would have been for an avalanche fatality, fueled rumors and suspicions about what had happened. You couldn't sit at a bar or in someone's garage without the hut trip coming up and blame being assigned. There were tales: Brett had put Cole in a tunnel that he built in the snow, then, when the entrance collapsed overnight, propped it up with his body, freezing to death. Brett had given his warm layers to Cole, including an insulating vest, which was why he was so lightly dressed. Cole, the wild boy, had skied into Porcupine Gulch first, causing Brett to chase after him and become trapped.

No one knew why Cole couldn't tell his story. Was it because he was doubly traumatized from his mother's death and now this? Was it due to survivor's guilt? Logic supported a combination of the two.

Some respected his silence, citing the innocence of a child; others believed Cari and their girls deserved to know everything Cole knew. *Just speak up, kid*, they thought.

It would have been easier if Cole were describing a purely heroic act, like the rumors suggested. But Cole couldn't say that.

Joel fielded questions all the time. Naccarato ran into him at the grocery store and asked how Cole was doing. "He's okay, he's getting through it," Joel said. Naccarato leaned in and whispered, "Did he ever tell you what happened?" "No," Joel replied, "he hasn't told me anything."

Joel privately conjured ways in. He approached Burkley before Cole got his physical. "Can you try and talk to him?"

Burkley obliged, but received the same answer.

"I'm good," Cole said.

Chuck floated down the San Juan River with Cole for six

hours one day, dissecting the fragility of life. Cole shared some of the lessons he'd learned—that it doesn't matter if you eat healthy and stay in shape and are spiritually aware; you can still be taken at any time. But when Chuck asked Cole if he wanted to discuss the hut trip, Cole said, "No, I'm doing fine," then changed the subject.

"What are we going to do?" Joel wondered.

"He'll talk," Chuck said, "when he's ready."

12

IS IT WORTH IT?

I learned of the Uncle Bud's tragedy in early 2019 from a friend who had also been buddies with Brett. He told me a version of the snow-cave tale: how Brett had shielded the boy from a blizzard overnight, costing him his life. It sounded like a heroic act, yet untold. But the mystery confused me, as it did others. My friend said nobody knew, two years later, how such a wilderness savant as Brett had gotten trapped in Porcupine Gulch. Why hadn't he and the boy been able escape?

The answer became clear later. When Cole's skins froze and Brett's scales failed to grip the deep, dry snow, their only hope of returning to the hut was to climb out on foot. If they had kept wallowing uphill, eventually they would have reached the rim of the gulch and been able to ski back to Uncle Bud's, even if it took twelve hours and drained their strength. But because they were disoriented, they didn't recognize this as a last resort. The moment they decided to descend deeper into the forest marked their point of no return. They also could have skied to Tennessee Flats and Highway 24, five miles east, but without a map, they had no idea that route existed.

Cole's silence, and the fact that Brett had left behind two children, came to haunt me. I kept thinking about how straightforward the outing sounded—zipping out for a quick powder run, something I, a frequent hut tripper and professional hutmaster, had done countless times—and how it devastated Brett's family, who, incredibly, still didn't know the full story. I had questions, both factual and existential. Chief among them: Is the adventure worth it?

—

I'd pondered that subject many times before I peered over an alpine ridge on the morning of April 26, 2022. A friend and I had climbed the shoulder of 13,684-foot Bald Mountain, or "Baldy," above our hometown of Breckenridge, Colorado.

I paused near the edge of a cornice—an overhanging shelf of snow—guarding the entrance to a steep one-thousand-foot tube so plump with powder it looked pregnant. A healthy storm cycle had just delivered fifteen inches of fresh snow, spread out over three days. The storm arrived with high winds and then turned calm, a rarity in our area. Lower-elevation slopes had entered a more predictable melt-freeze cycle, and avalanche activity seemed to have ebbed. After waiting all winter to ski steeper backcountry terrain, it felt like the time had come. I had texted the idea to my friend Liam, and he'd decided to join me. Our wives agreed to take our kids to school, which freed us to meet at the trailhead at 6:45 a.m.— early enough to beat the sun and warming temperatures.

I *wanted* the skiing to be as perfect as it had been here in the past: fresh powder flying over our heads under a blue-bird sky. So when I pulled up data from a nearby weather station at 12,500 feet, I tried to rationalize numbers that I knew contradicted my desire. Average wind speeds had increased overnight to thirty-three miles per hour, with gusts nearing forty—plenty strong enough to drift new snow into a leeward wind slab, which would increase the risk of a slide.

The Colorado Avalanche Information Center had rated the danger as "moderate" that morning (Level 2 on a five-point scale), with a plan to drop it to "low" the next day. "The lingering Persistent Slab avalanche problem is firmly on its way out," the forecast read, addressing the most unpredictable kind of slide, which runs on weak layers buried deep within a snowpack. The forecast noted it was still possible to trigger a persistent slab in "steep, rocky, thin, northerly facing areas."

We had skied our first run at 9:10 a.m., with temps in the teens and a steady wind blowing across the summit ridge at thirteen thousand feet. I had ski cut the top of the chute, slicing horizontally across the entrance to check for a wind slab—a smaller and less deadly hazard than a persistent slab—but found none. Liam and I took turns descending in dry powder, periodically stopping below rock outcroppings for safety.

We stood on top of the second run at 11:45 a.m. Though it started from roughly the same elevation as the first, it was significantly wider and had a more northerly aspect. A rocky rib separated our chute like an exposed black spine in the snow from a massive bowl to the left. But both features converged in a flat area at the base of the run, and anyone who has studied persistent-slab avalanches knows they can be triggered from far below the point where the snow fractures, like pulling out the leg of a heavy table. Though rarely seen in late April, a persistent slab killed five men on April 20, 2013, about twenty miles north of Baldy.

Liam dropped in first, testing the right edge of the slope for stability. As he did, I heard a sound like Styrofoam breaking and felt part of the cornice collapse a few feet in front of my ski tips, watching a wind slab about fifty feet wide drop away into the chute, triggered by his weight. The avalanche immediately picked up speed, with Liam on it. "Get right! Get right! Get right!" I yelled. He skied at a forty-five-degree angle toward a safe spot, high stepping at the last second to get off the moving snow. On its fringes the slab was only six inches deep, but in the middle, where it broke from the cornice, it was four to five feet thick. The weight of those sliding chunks—somewhere around thirty-five tons—set off a deeper avalanche, the first of three persistent slabs we were about to witness. The first gutted the center of the chute, not spreading outward; but when it reached the bottom, the entire left wall of the chute liquefied, sending a much larger mass racing to the flats below.

We watched that second wave smash the ascent track we'd put in after our first run, detonating over a depression and blasting powder high into the air. The first persistent slab hadn't been heavy enough to trigger the massive bowl to our left, but the weight of the second slide ripped out its under-lying support, causing it to collapse. The bowl broke across the entire rim one thousand feet higher, sending an almost in-conceivable tsunami of snow thundering down the mountain. The debris rumbled past where the earlier slides had stopped and continued for hundreds of yards into the flats.

The sequence lasted for more than a minute; the ava-lanches spanned a half-mile in width and left bare ground exposed. The entire season's snowpack—up to 10 feet deep in places—was gone. I called 911 to report the avalanche and that no one had been caught, then Liam climbed back up to the ridge, and we hugged. There was no doubt we would have died if we'd been caught in the first slide, be-cause the others buried its debris twenty feet deep.

We retreated down the ridge to Baldy's mellow frontside and skied back to our trucks. "You don't get another one of these," I said out loud to myself during the descent, still shak-ing. "That can never happen again. The alternative *has* to be enough."

I spent the next two days shoveling out my backyard and replaying what had happened, haunted by visions of the cornice taking me with it, or of Liam getting sucked into the churning debris. I pictured myself trying to excavate him, then, after I couldn't, standing on the snow waiting for a helicopter, distraught, crying, hating everything I'd ever been. I imagined telling his wife, seeing his two daughters, knowing *I* was the one to suggest we ski the backside of Baldy. In the versions where I had been caught and killed, I pictured my sweet sons, ages four and seven, crying in their mother's arms for years, knowing Daddy had died ski-ing powder and wondering whether he'd loved it more than them. For weeks, I went to bed hating myself. *Is this really what you want out of your life?*

"Things happen," my ski buddy Carl, sixty-three, told me as a means of reassurance. "They really do. We're lucky. We powder ski. It's amazing. Life is very delicate, but we're not going to sit in our houses being afraid."

I kept coming back to the rationale we use to evaluate even minimal risk. Weighing the odds that everything will work out, against the odds that your life will end, is pretty stress-free when the likelihood of the latter is, say, 10,000 to 1. But after you see a mountain fall away, you realize: Maybe the "1" should be viewed differently.

One month after our avalanche, on May 26, my wife, La-rissa, went for a trail run alone, leaving her cell phone in her car. Vomit Hill, so named for its steep, nausea-inducing climb, is a route she runs often each spring. It ascends from a popular trailhead for what feels like forever, the only relief coming in a wetland frequented by moose. (Although moose are usually indifferent to people, they can be extremely ag-gressive during the vernal calving season, and fatal attacks are not unheard of.) Just after crossing a log bridge, Lar-issa looked up to see a cow moose charging toward her at full speed. The beast smashed her like an NFL linebacker, chucking her into a clump of willows, where she assumed the fetal position and tried to protect her head. The moose stomped Larissa for nearly a minute, her screams echoing through an empty forest. Only after she stopped wailing did the cow relent and back away. Slowly Larissa rose to stand, covered in welts and hematomas from her shoulders to her ankles. She heard whimpering to her right and turned to see a freshly born calf stumbling toward her—the root of mama's fury. As she backed away down the trail, the calf started to follow, too new to know even what species it was. The mother noticed, and Larissa took off sprinting, the pain of her bruises temporarily numbed by adrenaline. She didn't stop until she reached her car.

A month and five days later, on July 1, our seven-year-old son Lachlan was riding his mountain bike on a gravel trail as part of a town-sanctioned camp. His front wheel washed out, pitching him forward like Superman. His face smashed into a boulder, stopping him cold. Four adult front teeth on his upper jaw were driven so far into his gums that we couldn't see them when we arrived at the emergency room, cradling our bloodied boy in our arms. We spent the night in two hospitals, terrified that the impact had damaged his brain. In the end he escaped with nineteen stitches, a broken jaw, and a years-long dental journey. We felt like we had won the lottery.

In the ensuing months I couldn't help but ponder our family's fate. All three close calls had stemmed from standard recreational activities in familiar places—stuff that we do every day. Any of them could have been fatal, or at least carried life-long consequences. Instead, we got lucky. Why? Could there ever be a reason why we were spared and Brett was not?

I concluded that the adventure is worth it only if it ends well. Then it can do what it does for us, lifting us up, enriching our lives, not stealing years of joy and love, as it does to us when it ends badly. But that is also life as a whole, and as the saying in these precious mountains lays bare, you never know unless you go.

—

Brett always wanted everyone to be excited about life. But it took his friends a while to find that again after he died. Some couldn't snowmobile for months. One didn't play his guitar for a year, because he had played it only with Brett. Their rallying cry was gone, like when a patriarch dies and the family stops coming together.

Perhaps most curious, however, was the way in which his death made them question themselves and the life they'd chosen.

"I ride differently than I did before," Chris Tracy admits. "Tentative. And I have this fear that that tentativeness is what will get me caught up. Because confidence gets you through."

Tracy, forty-four, learned long ago to live with the risk. After one of his riding partners, beloved SAR veteran Vern Kelso, died in an avalanche on Marshall Pass in 2010, Tracy kept Kelso's funeral program in his jacket pocket, "just to remind me: It can happen." But Brett's accident was rattling in its innocence. "It changed a lot of people's impression of the backcountry," Tracy says. "It's changed what I carry, changed my pretrip checklists and contact lists; I leave more detailed route descriptions of where we think we're gonna go. I bring multiple ways of starting a fire. Lighter and gas, cotton balls with Vaseline, and a bag of Fritos, which are one of the best starters anywhere. I always had a limb saw, but now I bring two, because they're that important. I make sure I have a primary clutch spring, ten-millimeter deep dish to get it out, two belts, all the little things that can break, heavy-duty zip ties, extra gloves, extra provisions." He doesn't always eat his roast beef and provolone sandwich for lunch, saving it until he gets back to the truck. "Just in case."

Tyler Lehmann, who was rebuffed in the parking lot after driving for seven hours to search for Brett, still considers Brett's death "an open wound." He's now a father of three boys and works as a logger. "I don't ski much anymore, I'm not climbing peaks, I haven't ridden a dirt bike in five years," he says. "Part of that is due to injuries; I messed up my legs, my shoulders, my hip, had surgery on my hand, and had to give up handlebars for a while. But I also choose not to put myself in the numbers game. Risk."

After Kurt Glaser watched Rob Walmer, his kayaking protégé, drown in the notorious Pine Creek rapid in 1997, he couldn't talk about what happened for two years. But he had no problem returning to big water. Later that season Glaser kayaked the Grand Canyon, the raucous Gauley River in West Virginia, and Gore Canyon, Colorado's king run. "I was still a charger," he says. "In one respect, I was like, 'Let's not pass this up.'" Then he thought about Walmer's age, thirty-two, and his own, twenty-seven. "I realized, if I live to the fullest, lighting it up and doing all the gnarly shit I'm doing, then I only have another five years. That made me pull back. I started telling friends, 'There's no shame in shouldering a rapid. If you don't feel comfortable, walk around it.'" He also repeated the lesson he learned in Pine Creek: "Chase people, not boats."

Few people in Brett's life rode the adventure like D-Bone. He dealt with stress like everyone but didn't let it derail his joy. Until he watched the tear weep out of Brett's eye and freeze to his cheek. Then nothing was ever the same.

He collected his sleeping bags that he'd wrapped Brett in, drove them to Grand Junction, and handed them to a shivering man outside a gas station. Skiing became too painful: He couldn't bear to see the skis Brett died on, let alone derive pleasure from them. Often he woke up sweating, his muscles sore from clenching, unable to remember anything from his dream except the image of Brett's tear, trickling down his skin. He never talked about the search but to his wife. Most people in town had no idea he'd even been there.

"It's still haunting," he said the first time we met, in the fall of 2022. "Even the wife told me, 'Don't let this interview bring up demons.' I was like, 'The demons are always there.'"

A year later, I bumped into him at a bar, and we made plans to ski at Monarch. "I've come a long way since then. I'm stronger now," D-Bone says. "I finally came to terms with the fact that we tried. I gave him the damn book, I showed him on the map, gave him better gear, then at the hut I showed him on the map again. That's all I can do."

Chris Burandt often asks his snowmobiling clients, over lunch in the wild, how many of them are carrying a fire starter. Then he tells Brett's story. "If nothing is learned from it, it's called a mistake," Burandt says. "If something is learned, it's called a lesson."

For those who still go, myself included, the question underlines our relationship with nature. Why do we forgive and accept its reconciliations, when it never utters a word? What is it in us—in it?

The answer is idiosyncratic. "What attracts me," Nate Porter says one day by the river, "is that nature is neutral. We assign it values sometimes, or even anthropomorphize it. But the fact is that the earth is what it is regardless of us. And maybe, subconsciously, that's the appeal: we don't get that in life very often. So much else has nuances and responsibilities or expectations—layers of things, emotions, that take away from purity of experience. But when you're out in nature doing your thing, whether you know it or not, that is such a pure form of connection with your inner self that I think that's why we do it."

"Think about everything Brett missed out on," his buddy Kurt Beddingfield says, wiping tears from his eyes. "And then go back to is it worth the risk. It wasn't a risk when he took it, but it's worth the risk. Life's worth the risk. Because if you don't, nothing happens."

■

The question of whether to reengage was significantly more complicated, however, for Brett's wife and daughters—the people who had lost the most to nature.

According to the limited psychoanalytic literature on bereaved adolescents, reviewed in *OMEGA: Journal of Death and Dying*, kids often keep their deceased parent in mind by "acquiring the habits and interests" that he or she loved. Bari didn't need to acquire anything from Brett when it came to the outdoors; it already lived within. She, like he, craved to be outside every minute of the day, using her body.

The first summer without him, Bari decided she needed to get away. A lot of things haunted her, none more than the regret she carried for not opening her eyes the morning her dad left for Uncle Bud's. *Why didn't I look at him?* She had read about people finding inner strength on long-distance treks and committed to hike the 567-mile Colorado Trail—alone. She set out shortly after her high-school graduation. For nearly a month she walked twenty miles a day, over mountain ranges and through thunderstorms, subsisting on rice and peanut butter. But no revelation came. Instead of growing in isolation, she realized she craved connection. "I felt even more trapped in my loneliness," she says.

Bari feared being on snow. It was one reason why she chose to attend Colorado Mesa University, in Grand Junction: because it was in the desert. She never talked about her dad's accident there. But it lurked. Her friend Abby invited her to go cross-country skiing almost two years after Brett's death. When they got to the trailhead, high on the Grand Mesa overlooking western Colorado, she felt her chest tighten. "I don't know if I can do this right now," she said. Still, almost trying to will it away, Bari joined CMU's Nordic ski team. She suffered "mini panic attacks" every time she skied, missing her dad. If someone asked what was wrong, she said, "Oh, nothing."

In June 2019, the Beasleys drove to Arizona to raft the

Grand Canyon: a respite from their grief. Bari and Brooke aimed to R2 the river, or run it as a duo in an eleven-foot rubber catamaran—a goal that held special meaning for Brooke, who had struggled with imposter syndrome since she was young and sought to prove she could do something strenuous and scary outdoors. It would be their first time down the Grand, a pinnacle journey that Brett never got to take. Though his absence made it emptier, it also symbolized their moving forward.

Cari didn't realize how dangerous the water was—massive waves that broke at all times. Bari and Brooke paddled their lightweight boat into the first serious rapid, Hance, at mile seventy-seven. One of the longest in the canyon, Hance features a series of keeper holes, a circulating pit that can trap boaters, known as the Land of the Giants—starting with Emilio's Hole at the top. At least four people have drowned after being flipped in Emilio's, including its namesake in 1994. The key to R2ing is a coordinated attack, and as Bari and Brooke entered the rapid, they lacked a plan. Emilio's sucked them in sideways and tossed their cat like a cork, ejecting them. Bari grabbed hold of the capsized boat and swam to shore halfway down. But Brooke wasn't as lucky. The frigid river pulled her under three times as she gasped for air, fearing for her life. A year later, Brooke would survive another harrowing swim, this time in a rapid near Salida named Seidel's Suckhole. It was her third traumatic experience in three years, starting with the hut trip. She felt as if the mountain life were pushing her away.

For Bari, however, the Grand Canyon trip marked a turning point. She realized that doing hard things in nature was what she wanted. In early 2020, she took an eight-week avalanche forecasting course in Driggs, Idaho—the only female among twenty participants. Part of their curriculum required them to analyze accident reports; Bari was surprised to find that didn't trigger a panic attack. Neither did their time in the field. She attributed the shift to her gaining control over an environment that had felt almost murderous up to then. She began wondering how she could make a living in it, just like her dad had done.

No one's relationship with adventure swung more than Cari's, however. After Brett died, she had turned to exercise, running for three hours a day. "It felt like my heart was beating so fast that I had to be moving to keep up with it," she says. "My chest would just ache. I couldn't eat or swallow. It felt like somebody was strangling me. My stomach clenched up for a year." She forced herself to down a handful of popcorn or a grapefruit, but the lack of nutrition made her shockingly skinny. After a while her hair started falling out in clumps. She was too weak to do gnarly things even if she'd wanted to.

Cari never piloted a boat while Brett was alive. It was easier to sit back and let him lead. After his death, however, saddled with all his gear, she decided it was time to figure it out for herself. She and a friend rafted the San Juan from Mexican Hat in the summer of 2017. For the first time, Cari realized she could do it on her own—rig a boat, read water, survive.

In early 2019, while out for beers after a mountain-bike ride, Cari and some friends agreed to form a women's masters rafting team and enter the national race later that summer in Salida. They practiced and won, qualifying for the world championships in China the next year. They trained four nights a week, paddling intervals in the pool, and sweated through gym workouts at dawn. Cari loved the torture as much as she loved being around strong, brave women, like her mother. "That's what I come from," she says, "and, I've realized, that's what I thrive on."

Cari conquered other challenges along the way. In 2021, she ran a trail marathon. In 2022, she biked the vaunted White Rim loop in Utah in a day—one hundred miles through the desert in twelve hours.

All of which led to a climactic moment on June 25, 2023. Butterflies flapped in Cari's stomach as she stared, horrified, at an ocean trying to squeeze through a crack. It was a few minutes before the start of the US Rafting Nationals down-river race. Teams of four prepared to run the Royal Gorge, the longest, wildest stretch of whitewater on the Arkansas River—a ten-mile gauntlet of almost continuous Class V rapids southeast of Salida, with twelve-hundred-foot rock walls towering above. Earlier in the week it had been un-clear whether the race would be allowed in the gorge, since it closes to boats if the flow eclipses 3,000 cubic feet per second. But the water settled at 2,860 cubic feet per second—too dangerous for commercial trips, which cease at 2,800, but runnable for the race.

Two days earlier, Cari's team, the Ark Aces, took a train-ing run. It didn't go well. They high-sided, or tipped to a point of nearly flipping in the scariest rapid, Sunshine

Falls. She had just come off the Grand Canyon, where the waves were even bigger—and where, for the first time, she rowed some of the rapids. Now, looking toward the dragon's mouth, Cari felt her stomach clenching. "I'm okay, I'm okay," she told herself. But she couldn't shake an ominous feeling. *Should I really be doing this?*

Cari's team aimed to shoot the gorge in just over an hour. The prospect of getting tossed into the river, with water temperatures in the fifties, carries lethal implications from hypothermia (submersion in water sucks heat from the body twenty-five times faster than air). Cari's quartet ranged in age from forty-five to fifty-eight; all were mothers and most had worked as professional raft guides. The night before the race, her teammate Samantha Bahn called a river ranger and requested additional support inside the gorge. Two safety boaters stood ready to assist with throw bags halfway down.

Bari and Brooke, especially Brooke, had worried about their mom as she courted new risks. Cari fretted about mortality, too. *What if I don't come back?* she thought before running the Grand Canyon. But she never considered not going, and, in a twist of irony, Brett's friends couldn't help but see his spirit coming out in her.

The race began. The Aces floated over a submerged car, which had rolled into the river a week earlier, and entered a sequence of rapids known as El Primero, El Segundo, and El Tercero—normally mere babies but that day comprising a wave train ten feet tall. The shoreline became a pile of sharp boulders as the canyon tightened and the eddies, or safe zones to pull out, disappeared. They entered Sunshine Falls, a trio of six-foot cliff drops that most boaters stop to scout. This time their line was perfect.

Whatever relief they felt evaporated as they hit the Graveyard, then Sledgehammer, where they paddled furiously to avoid a keeper hole on the right. Rocketing through a wave train called Hey Diddle Diddle (straight down the middle!), they were thrust into the Narrows, an exhilarating stretch of waves lined by rebar from the railroad that protrudes from shore. The Aces passed under the famous Royal Gorge Bridge, then navigated Wall Slammer and the menacing Boat Eater rock, after which they were spit out like a watermelon seed for a mad paddle to Cañon City.

They had achieved their primary goal—staying alive—while finishing only seven minutes behind the much younger Open Women champs. Their victory qualified them for the 2024 Worlds in Bosnia.

"I always think when I'm doing something, *Would I be doing this if Brett were here?*" Cari told me later. "Then my other thought in the gorge was, *Am I going to orphan my kids?* That's on my mind most of the time. But if I didn't do this stuff, I don't think the girls would be proud of me. Brett was the cool and adventurous parent, and I felt a sense of responsibility to uphold that—be someone they're proud of and excited to tell their friends about. I think that drives me. And it feels *so* good when you accomplish it."

That day, at least, the adventure had been worth the risk.

13

DAWN

Grief was harder to navigate than nature. Instead of two roads to take—returning to the wild or abstaining—the ways in which we process and, we hope, survive another's death are endless.

Brett's parents, Bob and Liz, were in Florida when Cari called to break the news. Bob, known for his stoicism, bawled like no one had ever seen him cry, convulsing like a child. "Just a shell," his daughter Brie says. "Mom and I didn't know how to fix him."

They decided not to attend their son's memorial service in Salida. Seven years later, I asked why. Bob paused. "I guess I just couldn't bear it at the time," he says. "I didn't know how I'd handle it. I didn't want to have any outbursts against anyone for letting him go up there in a snowstorm." The pastor mailed them a video of the service, but they couldn't watch that, either.

I had flown to meet them at their home in New Smyrna Beach, where they live in a golf-course development. Photos of Brett hung in their den. The accident remained an enigma. Bob, eighty-five, says he understood that at the hut that day, "the kid left, and when Brooke realized that he was gone, she told her dad to help, and he went after the kid."

I explained that Brett and Cole actually left the hut together. "Oh, okay. Well, somehow this kid went the wrong way, I'm told."

"I totally believe that Brett saved his life," adds Liz, who is eighty. "And the reason I believe that is because that is what Brett would do. It's hard to understand that Brett would take the wrong . . . I mean, I had heard the kid was a little ahead of him and Brett followed him down. But that may not be true. Maybe he didn't save the kid's life."

"Well, he did," Bob says.

"The kid lived and didn't have anything wrong, and Brett died," Liz concludes. "Hopefully he will go on and do something good with his life."

"To Brie and I," she adds, "Brett was still alive, he was just in Colorado, and it wasn't a reality to us because we were not there. That's why I can't go back. I know I gotta get past that. We're denying it. I mean, I know he's gone."

Brie expounds later: "Mom and I kinda live in a fantasy world. In our minds, Brett's just on vacation. And it works. We're afraid if we see his house and Cari and Bari and Brooke, then it will hit us. So I will never go to Colorado. And that's just how I keep myself sane. I tell all my friends who are dealing with stuff, 'Just do what Mom and I do.'"

None of Brett's four siblings ever visited him in Salida. But the place came to represent something sacred to his sister Beverly, who was twelve years older. She didn't know Brett as a kid; he was part of "the other side"—Bob's second family. But they connected as adults, and after Brett died, something about the life he lived left her pining to be close to him. She learned that a trail had been renamed "Beasway" in his honor and decided that was where she would spend eternity. "I told my kids, I want to be cremated and have my ashes mixed with dirt, then I want you to take me to Colorado and lay me in the forest," she says.

—

On Brett's birthday the first few years after his death, a group of men gathered at Ed Trail's house. They drank Brett's favorite beer, Busch Light, shot fireworks over the golf course, and called friends who had moved away, leaving the phone on speaker for hours. Trail owns Brett's '95 Harley and has "BB" tattooed on his arm. Others keep his photo on their refrigerator; it's common in Salida to see "BB" stickers on bikes. Friends adopted his traits: making sure to acknowledge others in public, striving to be inclusive, and forgiving the weirdness in people, because, as Brett often said, "Who isn't weird?"

Naccarato was one of the few who saw a counselor. "I got really hung up on why the fuck didn't he have a lighter?" he recalls, crying. "I really struggled and I thought back on numerous adventures when Brett wasn't prepared. And I was mad at him for a while. That's a normal stage of grief. I was pissed that he left his wife and daughters, left his friends. Like, I could see him start pacing when people said they would be ready to go, because I've seen it before. When he was ready to go, it was time to go."

LCSAR reevaluated its operations in the wake of what happened. Its snowmobiles are higher powered now, with volunteers trained to ride them in complex terrain. Its roster is five times larger and substantially younger. Members attend an annual hypothermia training where Brett's accident serves as the primary case study. "The team that responded to that incident back in 2017 is not the team we have today," LCSAR president Becky Young says. "Literally and logistically and financially." (Still, no incident report exists from the Uncle Bud's mission, Young says, and the team wasn't mandated to write one, which surprised me, especially for a fatality.)

LCSAR wasn't the only governmental organization that looked in the mirror afterward. The Salida Ranger District did too. Brett's void was chasmic, both operationally and culturally. District Ranger Jim Pitts tried to hire a replacement. It didn't work out. After a year, the district split Brett's job into two full-time positions.

How someone so obsessed with safety had made such basic errors confounded Brett's co-workers, especially those who worked for him. "His death wrecked my world for a really long time," says Dani Cook, his former OHV crew leader and now the trail coordinator for the San Isabel National Forest. "Just, why did he do this? If he teaches every time we go out to be this prepared, how the fuck did this happen?" Eventually she came to a conclusion. "The way I accepted it is, there's work mode and there's play mode. I think he preached so much safety that he needed to let loose, and not be the one always preaching."

For the district safety awards the year he died, Cook built survival kits for the winners that included enough to be okay for three days in the wild. They fit in her hand and cost less than fifty dollars. "Because it was traumatizing to think he went out so unprepared," Cook says.

—

Joel, who struggled to forgive Brett for taking his son along with him, who couldn't turn off the GIF in his head, eventually learned to let go. "The hut trip doesn't have as much power over me as it did," he says in his living room, overlooking the Ark. His cancer, which he treated with a combination of immunotherapy and chemotherapy, remained in remission. "Right afterward, I was so amped up. I can look back and say maybe I was a little overbearing when I was talking with Cari. I probably should've just backed away."

One of the ways in which he coped was by reading survival stories. They informed his takeaway and brought peace. "Sometimes the most experienced people end up taking shortcuts at inappropriate times, and sometimes they get bit," he says. The inferences are impossible to ignore, yet the emotion behind them is more neutral than it was. "Nobody's to blame," he adds. "We all bear some responsibility for how that happened."

One summer morning Joel and his girlfriend, Tracey,

went hiking on the Continental Divide, intending to complete a ten-mile loop above tree line. The weather forecast was perfect. But shortly after noon, clouds encroached and the sky darkened, as often happens in Colorado. Frightened and wanting to be lower where their exposure was less, they bushwhacked down the mountain, ending at a popular destination called Waterdog Lakes. Joel and his kids had staged a memorial for Laurie at Waterdog Lakes, spreading her ashes and placing keepsakes in a small shrine in the forest. Most of the items were gone, but as Joel restacked some of the rocks they had piled up, he found one of Laurie's tarot cards, preserved under a hunk of talus. Its title was "Truth." The message read: "What is is. What is not is not. No amount of wishing or wanting can change it. It's that simple."

—

Cari didn't know if she would ever find another partner, but eventually she felt ready. Her friends, attempting to cheer her up, had helped her make a list of traits she sought. Almost as a joke, with a Grand Canyon trip approaching the year after Brett's death, Cari included: "Be able to row down the Grand."

One night in February 2018, she met a tall, bearded ski patroller at Benson's Tavern. Aaron Robbins, 43, had moved to Salida nine months earlier and happened to be an expert oarsman, as well as a Grateful Dead devotee and musician. That night, he was playing bass in a duet. Brett had always told Cari, "When you find a bass player, never let him go, because every band needs a bass player." She felt like he had given her his blessing, like meeting Aaron was meant to be. They soon fell in love. Aaron let her cry until her eyes were dry. Talking about Brett didn't bother him.

Years later, they decided to build a house near Methodist Mountain south of town. Cari had turned Brett's 1971 VW bus into an informal temple when he died, storing his personal mementos inside as she cleaned out their home on H Street. Now, the bus lived in their new yard, parked among piñon pines. Brett had never journaled or left much of a paper trail, so the contents of the bus offer as intimate a peek into his mind as anything.

One sunny fall morning, Cari met me to look through it. She'd refused to get rid of Brett's keepsakes until Bari and Brooke had a chance to decide what to toss, which they weren't ready to do. So the bus remained a time capsule. Someday Aaron planned to fix up the interior and pass it on to them, like he'd done with Brett's raft, *Peely Dan*.

One of the first photos I picked up was of Brett, tan and young, shirtless and smiling, leaning toward a laughing, infant Bari in the bathtub, their eyes locked together. A newspaper photo showed the girls at ages five and two, carrying a trash bag on town cleanup day. Both were golden blond; Bari's hair was pulled back in braids with a red barrette. "I want to talk to them and remember what their little voices sound like," Cari says, studying the photo.

Bari had looked through the bus contents before, Cari says, but "Brooke didn't want anything to do with this."

Wedged between a CPR face shield and Brett's black and

white dirt-bike helmet were stacks of paper, including photos that he had printed at work. A strip that he had cut out and kept in his office read: "Live as if you were to die tomorrow. Learn as if you were to live forever." Another said, "Worrying doesn't take away tomorrow's troubles, but it does take away today's peace."

The images captured his life: Brett in firefighting gear and a yellow hard hat with the forest floor ablaze a few feet away. Brett wearing waders and netting a monster rainbow trout. A collage from Grateful Dead shows, of which he attended thirty; backpacking trips; Brett with dreads and Cari looking fifteen; Bob the dog wandering in the ocean.

Cari held up a framed portrait of her and Brett with Bob as a puppy. She didn't say anything; she just looked at it for a while.

Brett, Cari, and Bob the dog in 1994.

"I want to thank you for allowing me to come to Salida and work for you," read a card from one of Brett's employees. "You're the coolest boss I've had."

Only a few sayings were deemed worthy of a full page by Brett, but this was among them: "People will forget what you said. People will forget what you did. But people will never forget how you made them feel."

A foam sword rested on his camp chair, next to three skateboards, a huge bag of koozies, and "Brett's penalty box rulebook" from roller derby. He'd saved an undated Father's Day card from each girl:

Thanks for being the coolest dad ever, and for taking me on so many fun things like mountain biking, rafting, etc. Thanks again for always supporting me in everything I do and for all the things you do for us. Love, Bari

I love you so so so so so so so so so so so so so so so so so so so so so so so so so much! I hope your day has been and will be fun! Love, Brooke

On a small square piece of paper, a list with instructions: "Do each of these things for a half-hour at least once a day, and you're sure to have a healthy, happy life."

1. Get the blood really pumping.
2. Let the sun shine directly on your skin.
3. Express yourself to someone.

4. Be creative.
5. Stretch.
6. Close your eyes and breathe deeply in through the nose and out through the mouth while letting your mind rest.
7. Think of the good things in your life.
8. Turn off the cellphone and close the computer.
9. Go for a walk.
10. Write something down . . . anything.

One more strip read: "The most basic of all human needs is the need to understand and be understood. The best way to understand people is to listen to them."

"Brett and I talked a lot about listening," Cari explains. "He would find somebody who he admired, and be like, what are they doing that draws people to them? And almost always he could come down to, they're just good listeners."

Cari kept Brett's ashes in a small, dusty urn in their home, near where his Forest Service hard hat hung on the wall. "I talk to him and apologize to him because I feel bad that he's in this box," she says. "I keep thinking I want to make some kind of glassware for the girls, with some of his ashes. But I get so much comfort that his whole him is in here."

For years she had searched for a note from Brett. Not a specific one, just something, anything, that would speak to her once more. She had given up and decided that such a thing didn't exist. Then one day while moving books from her nightstand, a slip of paper fell out. It read:

> CARI—
> I LOVE YOU SO SO MUCH—THANKS FOR
> BEING MY FRIEND—
>   xOXoXXxxOoo

She had reached a stage where she could be sad that Brett died but happy with her life, a prospect that had been unimaginable before. "I have to think it's part of our survival," Cari says. "You're able to move past that and have still more happiness. When I see people who are dwelling on the pain all the time, I'm like, that's really sad. There are so many great things. You just gotta keep going forward."

—

The research on bereaved adolescents doesn't tell you about their long-term life. It doesn't show how broken kids shimmy out of their caverns to become inspiring adults. In the summary published in *OMEGA*, almost all of the social, psychological, and behavioral effects reported by and observed in grieving children were negative. But a pair of studies noted positive outcomes, including an increase in resilience, accelerated maturity, and greater independence: One teen stated that "suffering makes you learn a lot about life, about yourself, about others, about everything—it makes you grow."

Bari, like Brooke, attended college on a full academic scholarship. She studied constantly at CMU, striving to outdo her classmates and maintain straight A's. But pressure to project a perfect image affected her eating habits. She started starving herself, self-harm spurred, she believes, by grief from losing her father.

Her hair thinned and eventually fell out. Anemia prevented her muscles from getting enough oxygen. Legs that had once run thirty miles at a time could barely make it through a 5K.

Bari attended three colleges in three years, eventually finishing at Western Colorado University in Gunnison, near Crested Butte. During her transience, she learned to be kind to herself, and she began speaking more openly about her anorexia. Her body healed and grew strong again. In 2021, the year after she graduated, she joined Crested Butte's ski patrol. The job paid her to rescue tourists and ski powder at one of the steepest resorts in the country. It also gave her a meaningful path to forge a career on snow.

I met her for a morning of skiing during her second season there, in late March 2023. Tall and confident, with long blond hair streaming out of her helmet and a weathered red and black ski patrol jacket, Bari stood at the top of Crested Butte's Spellbound Bowl, surveying her options. Repeated atmospheric rivers from the Pacific had fed one of the deepest winters on record—more than 320 inches of snow. We studied the radical basin before us: plummets in every direction, some more precipitous and airy than the rest. Bari decided to traverse right toward the Phoenix Chutes. We passed by a number of descents that would be steep and tight enough for most experts, finally stopping above a pair of twisting shafts. She dropped in and snapped her tails back and forth like windshield wipers, carving through the forested choke all the way to the bottom. Then she hopped off a four-foot rock and tucked toward the flats to gain speed.

The more time Bari spends in Crested Butte, the better she understands why her dad was drawn to Colorado. "I see the beauty in the mountains and how much he loved them. It makes me want to never leave," she says. "Also, on a personal level, yeah, the nature is amazing, but it's also scary and destructive and doesn't care about our lives. I think that's one thing I like about the patrol community, is they're very aware of that thin line. A lot of them have lost friends. I appreciate the level of precaution."

In a few days Crested Butte would close, and the other season in Bari's life would start. She had scored four hard-to-get whitewater permits in western Colorado and Utah in April and May, then, in June, she and Cari were rafting the Grand Canyon together—a gauntlet that Bari, a gifted oarswoman, would mostly row herself. After that, she'd return to guide the Taylor River and coach kids on mountain bikes until ski season started again.

She sent an email after her first trip, through Westwater Canyon on the Colorado. "It was everything you could imagine a spring river trip might be," she wrote. "Sunshine, snow, hail, 70 mph winds and scary high water. We had a blast."

Brooke would never equate scary conditions and physical suffering with joy. She used to want to, no matter the cost to her soul. Sometimes when Brett was alive, she looked at her friends' dads who were less adventurous and not as fun, but who were around all the time. *What would that be like?* she wondered. After he died, with Bari away at college and Cari struggling to parent because of her own grief, Brooke felt she was raising herself.

As high school went on and Cole reclaimed his confidence, Brooke saw a popular, outgoing kid who seemed to have nothing weighing him down, let alone the albatross she carried. Cole spun donuts in the parking lot, made people laugh, and led student cheers at sporting events. He partied on weekends and was easy to talk to. It seemed to Brooke that the accident hadn't affected him, that he didn't care that her dad had died. She was pretending to be okay in many of the same ways, but Cole's detachment felt too real to be fake. Every time she asked how he was, he simply said, "Good!"

How can you possibly just be good? she thought.

Brooke hid in her room, watching movies, playing music, numbly scrolling through social media, alone. To feel close to her dad, she listened to the Grateful Dead and replayed their conversation from the drive to the hut.

She wasn't ready to face the shame and regret that bored into her brain, insisting she had been a bad daughter for pushing him away, as teenage girls often do to their dads. *Oh my gosh. That's all the time you had and you wasted it*, she thought. If she spoke those fears to a therapist, it would mean they were true.

Brooke had used food as a salve in grief; eating was one of the few things that made her feel better. She had also yearned to be fit and strong her whole life, like the rest of her family. So when she got to college, she started purging and overexercising. Her hair fell out. "My body was in such a state of constant trauma, constant anxiety, constant panic. And that was the only way to release," Brooke says.

Her bulimia, she says, was "self-punishment, because of all the guilt I carried from the whole experience. I just felt so lost in my own body that I couldn't even think about what I wanted to do with my life. It was my way of suffering in silence. I never had to show it to anyone, which was comforting."

When I first met Brooke, at a coffee shop on a frigid morning in December 2022, she wore dark sunglasses for the interview. In two days, she would graduate a semester early from CMU with a 4.0 GPA. But all she could think about was who wouldn't be at the ceremony: her dad. She had gone to a friend's wedding recently, and when it was time for the father-daughter dance, she lost it. She ran outside, bawling, and FaceTimed Bari. "I don't even know if I can go to my own wedding," she says, forcing a smile through tears.

Bari still had never broached the hut trip with Brooke— what actually happened at Uncle Bud's. She didn't want to make her sister relive it. Brooke had her own reason for not bringing it up. The final twenty-four hours she'd spent with her dad were sacred, a memory that belonged to no one else. Despite their tight bond, Brooke still gets jealous of Bari for having known their dad better and having spent more time with him in his happy places, outside.

She couldn't bring herself to listen to his voicemails, which she refused to delete. But she sent me photos of his cards that she'd saved, many of which included little stick-figure people making funny faces.

BROOKE—YOU ARE SO SPECIAL—I LOVE
EVERYTHING ABOUT YOU—DAD XOXO

I'M LOOKING FORWARD TO HANGING
WITH YOU LATER—YOU MAKE ME SO
PROUD—I LOVE YOU SOOOOO MUCH. LUV,
DAD

A year and a half later, we met again, this time at a restaurant in Golden, near Denver, where Brooke had moved to start a life of her own. She had long dark hair, deep blue eyes, and creases in her cheeks like her dad's. She told me what she had been hiding at the coffee shop: that she'd agreed that morning to enter inpatient treatment for bulimia. For three months she lived at the Eating Recovery Center Colorado, through Christmas, in sweatpants, in rooms without mirrors, undergoing intensive therapy for trauma that had, unbeknownst to even her mother and sister, turned her existence into a slow form of suicide.

"I essentially had to beg my mom to go, because I was so good at putting on a face," Brooke says. "I was like, 'I don't want to live like this. I know how cool life can be, and I know how happy I can be. I'm so tired of being mean to myself. I'm not being mean to myself anymore. And I need help.'"

She couldn't use any of the numbing tactics she'd used in college, like getting blacked-out drunk. "I think it was freeing, honestly, to go to those dark places," she says. "Yes, you're really fucking sad that you're missing out on all these years with him. And you have regrets because you didn't act a certain way toward him, or didn't spend more time with him. Yes, you can cry about it. And then, eventually, this really sad moment will pass. I remember one day just bawling. It felt so good to bawl, because I didn't cry for so long. And it felt good to my dad, because for years I pretended I was fine, and then I felt shame that I hadn't cried about it."

Cari joined Brooke for family counseling sessions at the center. Brooke was able to say that her mom's constant invitations and encouragement to seek out adventure, though well-meaning, made Brooke feel inadequate—an admission she had hidden forever. The sessions helped Brooke realize that she was enough, that her mother would love her regardless.

In recovery, Brooke also embraced the mountain life that her dad had instilled in her, albeit a less intense version. She got into rock climbing and started mountain biking and skiing again—feeling close to her father whenever she went.

Her healing transformed their family. The baby, who kept everyone so worried, who declined help for years, suddenly was showing Cari and Bari that transparency could be empowering.

"It allowed me to be more open about things that I did while I was grieving that I'd kept tucked away, because it was embarrassing to bring them up," Bari says. She meant the eating disorders. "We were both doing it, and our mom too, but we were hiding it. Brooke broke that barrier. Her having the confidence to say that in front of us made us realize we were not alone."

Brooke's confidence extended to the hut trip itself. The first few times she drove past Leadville Junction, she flew by like a jet. Then one day she stopped and faced it: the scene of her greatest misery. "I was like, this spot isn't significant at the end of the day. It is, but it doesn't have to be," she says. "It's not fair to that mountain, that hut, to hold so much resentment. Because I could never go back to Leadville and probably be fine. But that doesn't do anything for me, for my dad. And it's a beautiful place."

In August 2024, Brooke started a mental-health counseling master's program at Adams State University with a focus on therapy. Her interest took root during her treatment. "It's the first time I've felt I know what I want to do with my life," she says, beaming. The father in me wished Brett could hear her—see her.

One of the trickiest elements of the Beasleys' reckoning, and Salida's, was viewing Brett in full, instead of through a rosy lens. Shortly after the accident, Cari hated hearing people make him out to be a deity, when she was left holding the wreckage of his fallibility. She couldn't express this to her girls, who needed their dad to stand on death's pedestal, at least at first. But in private, she told close friends, "I just want to scream, 'He wasn't perfect! Stop making it seem like he was perfect!'"

More recently, Cari has opened up to her daughters about her marital struggles with Brett—a microcosm of their journey as a family. "I saw that as a kid," Brooke says. "I saw the fights, the late nights, how anxious he would get and the effect on her. A lot of their arguments were about him feeling sad that someone didn't like him. So for her to express it is good. He was so glorified for so long, and that was how it had to be. Of course we were all sad, but it didn't feel as real. Now, we're actually talking about this real person. It's gotten so much better. Like, no bullshit."

14
FREED

A window into a lone survivor's soul often reveals profound loneliness and suffering—the crushing result of entering as two and leaving as one. But the survivor's burden and the manner in which that manifests depend greatly on the circumstances involved.

After the 1986 car crash in Salina, Kansas, that killed Brett's friend Bart Kline, much of the community vilified Lance Hassler. Those hit hardest by the tragedy were among the exceptions. "Brett never held Lance responsible," his sister Brie says. Instead, Brett blamed himself. "If I would've been there, I would've been driving," he said. The Klines made a point of greeting Lance at Bart's funeral and hugging him. They never sued or gave public statements about Lance, nor did they push for harsher criminal charges. Joann Kline, Bart's mother, wrote Lance a letter nine months later, telling him the crash was an accident and that she hoped he would have a good life. Bart's brother, Brent, and Lance became friends.

Lance, however, could not forgive himself. He drank heavily throughout adulthood and often woke up crying. "It should have been me," he told his wife, Layla, years later. "Bart should be here." He didn't believe he had a right to be happy or to enjoy his family, because Bart couldn't. "Lance was *tortured* by it," Layla says.

Two days after Thanksgiving 2004, Lance, by then divorced and living alone, died from the effects of alcoholism. His daughters were five and seven years old. The crash had claimed a second victim, eighteen years later.

The pain of surviving had been too much to overcome.

———

Plenty of people wondered how Cole's survival would affect him as he grew older. My first glimpse of that came five years later, on Wednesday, January 5, 2022: Brett's birthday. I met Cole at Alpine Park in Salida, sitting across from him at a picnic table. He was a twenty-year-old freshman at Montana State in Bozeman, six feet tall and a solid 155 pounds.

Cole had never told anyone his story. He began by describing what happened, from the moment he and Brett left the hut to when he was rescued, drawing a map to help me understand. It became clear that he still was confused about where they'd been.

Enduring the aftermath was almost as hard as enduring "my night out," as he called it. "I definitely felt a sense of embarrassment for becoming a liability and having to be found," he said. As for his silence: "I just preferred to continue to think about it for a while before I said anything. Also, it affected me, but it mostly affected Brett. So I felt weird telling his story."

"Did Brett ever apologize?" I asked.

"There wasn't really anything to apologize for, I thought," Cole said. "I mean, I felt responsible too. We both just wanted to get out and ski."

Part of what he gained from his mother and Brett, he explained, was an understanding of death: abstruse, unsparing, final. "A lot of it," he said, locking eyes with me, "is you just never know when you're going to go."

The following winter, I flew to Bozeman to interview Cole again. We skied two days at Bridger Bowl, a jagged ski area north of the city, and spent hours talking at a dog park near his apartment. One day Cole addressed his complicated relationship with Brooke. Contrary to how it appeared, he said, his crush hadn't dissipated after Brett's death. He just couldn't get past a dire scenario: Suppose he and Brooke dated for a while and it didn't work out, and he was the one who ended it. What would it look like if the boy who'd watched her dad die then broke her heart? It was too much to even consider, far-fetched or not, and the easiest solution—the safest—was to avoid it. Which, of course, came across as disaffection to her. He said he had wanted to talk to her for years, about everything. But he hadn't yet worked up the nerve.

The reason why he'd lived and Brett had died manifested in his mind practically: "I had a lot more clothes." But that didn't eliminate his guilt. "Just being the one who survived," Cole said, "there was something that I instantly correlated with, like, if you survived and somebody else didn't, they probably didn't survive because of you. Which is a very odd interpretation, but for some reason it made sense in a setting like that. Especially my decision to, subconsciously or consciously, not go back; I think that really haunted me the most. By then, I kind of knew, but I didn't. There was no proof. So, it's like, if I go back, would Brett not have died? That was the only thing I could have done differently."

On our third morning together, we went backcountry skiing in Hyalite Canyon, a popular zone south of where he lived. Conditions were warm and calm, and we expected to be out for only ninety minutes. Cole carried a reflective blanket, a lighter in a dry bag, a down jacket, hand and foot warmers, ample water, and enough food to last a day. "My mom used to tell me, 'You can always shed a layer,'" he said of his thicker wardrobe, starting up the frozen skin track. "I came to Bozeman and people were like, 'Oh, be bold, start cold.' That is the complete opposite of anything I've ever heard."

We topped out on a knoll with sprawling views. The snow was refrozen crud, as challenging as it gets. Cole, who had recently begun landing back flips, caught an edge halfway down and crashed. He stood up grinning. Seeing his comfort, and hearing him describe his outings with friends, I realized that backcountry skiing was not just a hobby for him. It was an essential part of his life, innocent still.

On a sunny afternoon the following July, I arrived to pick up Cole from his dad's house in Salida, a big-windowed modern with an apartment over the garage that Cole was renting for the summer. He had just turned twenty-two. We were planning to hike into Porcupine Gulch and camp, the first time Cole had returned since the accident. He met me outside with Tikka, his faithful cattle dog, dirty blond hair poking out from his baseball cap and a scruffy beard covering his face. He heaved his enormous pack into my truck and we headed north toward Leadville.

Cole has a thing about going back to correct a mistake. If he flips while rafting, he runs the rapid again as soon as possible. Porcupine was different, however. Returning meant confronting horrors he had worked hard to leave behind.

We reached Uncle Bud's Hut in my truck after lurching up the rutted dirt road that Cole and Brett had skied in 2017. We split up our food, then started hiking through the forest toward the saddle.

Just below Whiskey Knob, in a clearing that bore a striking resemblance to where he and Brett had dropped in six years earlier, Cole said, "Right here looks pretty damn familiar." Soon we intersected the Continental Divide Trail, which cut across the rim of the gulch before diving down toward Porcupine Creek. We descended to a switchback, and Cole eyed the steep hillside above us. It was more open than the rest of the forest and sloped like a ramp. "Now *that* looks familiar," Cole said: likely where they'd tried to hike up the first day, wallowing in sugar snow, before descending deeper into the gulch and becoming trapped.

When we reached the point where we'd leave the trail and begin to bushwhack, retracing their path down the drainage, we dropped our packs and continued up another rise to a stunning plateau, just to check it out. I had happened upon this site the prior year, when I'd hiked in to Porcupine on my own. Peaking wildflowers—purple and yellow and pink and red, waving in the wind—surrounded a lily pad lake. We ate fancy cheese and sliced apples while gaping at Galena Peak under a bluebird sky.

Cole and Tikka on the rim of Porcupine Gulch.

We returned to our packs and started down the creek bed, hiking overland now, as Cole and Brett had done on skis. Thick timber slowed our pace. We came across an old, crumbling lean-to built against an eight-foot-tall boulder and surrounded by rusty cans. Its floor was rotting; splintered walls had fallen in—likely an abandoned hunter's camp. How much it might have helped Brett and Cole was hard to say, but it almost certainly would've insulated them better than their crater.

Roughly a half mile after leaving the trail, we encountered a wide meadow at 10,500 feet elevation—1,100 vertical feet below the saddle. After consulting topographic maps with Chris Burandt and Jimmy Dalpes, who was part of D-Bone's search team and knows the area well, this meadow was my best guess as to where Burandt found Brett. We gazed out at a swaying sea of knee-high grass, pocked by clumps of willows. Tikka chased field mice, bouncing up and down like a hare, invisible one moment, airborne the next.

Cole brought up the TV series *Survivor*, which his roommates watch. He wondered aloud whether he could cut it on the show, without offering a reason. Despite the trauma of this place, he seemed relaxed, untriggered. He still gives himself often to nature; this summer he ran the Royal Gorge at twenty-five hundred cubic feet per second and, for the first time, Pine Creek, the rapid where Rob Walmer had died (albeit at a lower flow than that which trapped Walmer). Nature's bottom line is never far from his mind. "Like the bees when you're going to get honey—you might get stung," he said.

His flashbacks to his time with Brett don't cast the place as the villain, but instead focus on the circumstances of their ordeal—the mistakes and the mystery. Cole is perfectly comfortable being by himself in the mountains. Often when he reaches the top of an ascent, he sits and reflects for thirty minutes or so. "I don't think I can associate nature with being a monster," he said in the meadow.

We pitched our tents and built a small fire ring with rocks. A pile of kindling crackled to life. The light faded; stars peeked out around a half moon to the south. We were likely the only humans for miles. I tried to keep the conversation light, not wanting Cole to drift too far from the moment, where demons could lurk. I wished I could pry open his brain and read his thoughts.

"Think you'd ever come back here for catharsis?" I asked.

"Nah, I'd probably go to that lake where we stopped for food," he replied, referring to the lily pad pool earlier in the day. "Leave this place for Brett."

He pointed out the Big Dipper and Orion's Belt as he tended to the fire. A few times he laughed. Porcupine Creek gurgled fifty feet away.

The next morning, we hiked three hundred yards down the drainage into a much larger meadow, hopping over the creek to dodge deadfall and impenetrable brush. Mosquitoes swarmed as we plodded through hip-high monkshood, a purple flower that thrives in wet, subalpine marsh. The muddy grass slurped our shoes like suction cups.

In the northwest corner of the meadow, Cole stopped. "This definitely looks like it. I imagine I just followed the creek straight through, and Burandt rode up right here." Birds chirped. Squirrels darted. Cole glanced around the clearing, where his life had been saved. There was no grand conclusion or revelatory quote. Only silence for a minute.

The following day, while we were driving down Uncle Bud's Road, Cole said, "Going back was something I needed to do. I wouldn't have gone on my own."

The captivity of being lost echoed, still, and begged a question: Are we ever in control in nature? Or do we just feel that way when it lets us?

"It's a sense of power," Cole said. "You just question yourself. You never have full confidence in the choices you've made or are making. Like, do you *want* to take that extra step? Are you benefiting yourself, or not?

"There was a part of me that felt relieved to come back and be the one in power, rather than have the place be in power."

—

In mid-January 2024, I return to Monarch with Cole for one last ski day. It's the middle of a potent storm cycle, and the slopes are covered in a quilt of white fluff. The air, however, is minus-eleven degrees, and the gusting wind burns our cheeks the moment we leave my truck—creating a summit wind chill that is forty below zero. Only a handful of people are out skiing, but Cole, home from college on winter break, is undaunted.

In a few days he will return to Montana, where he is majoring in exercise science. Though he gets cold more easily since the hut trip, and though he still skis in the same boots, his extremities are comfortable at the moment, as we shield our faces from the arctic sting.

We get off the Panorama lift and start skating up an incline toward a corniced stash called Curecanti, Cole in front. It's a shortcut of sorts that crosses a plane of virgin snow. As we shuffle along, out of view of people and with no civilization in sight, I can't help but think of the symbolism: the boy who followed a forty-something dad into the white abyss, almost to his death, now a strong and capable man, leading me, another forty-something dad, into a similar image, drawn, once more, by joy. When we drop in, the snow explodes in Cole's face, and I capture the moment in a photo. All you can see are his poles.

I have come to ski with Cole, but also to clarify some details that have arisen since our last meeting. Both Chris Burandt and LCSAR incident commander Anita Mason said Cole told them the day he was rescued that Brett had instructed him to "keep going," which was why they'd separated—why Cole had left Brett behind. Yet when I'd asked Cole in Montana if he remembered Brett saying that, he'd said no. Additionally, Cole had told me he never saw Brett fall, a statement that contradicted his father's newspaper account and what Joel had told me. I'm curious whether he blacked out those facts, lost the memories to time, or whether there is a different explanation.

During our drive down the mountain, I ask again: "Did Brett tell you to keep going?"

Cole inhales deeply. "I'm pretty sure Brett didn't say it," he says. "And the reason I would've said that is to justify leaving him."

Suddenly I don't see a twenty-two-year-old man. I see a fifteen-year-old child, scared, freezing, trying to explain an inexplicable tragedy. I see a boy who had just watched his mother die, who knew death to look a certain way, gradual and calm and quiet, yet now had been tasked with assessing the signs of death in a man one who'd appeared invincible hours earlier, until nature began to consume him. A boy who had tried to save himself but didn't know whether he'd been allowed to.

I see, in full for the first time, the startling guilt of a lone survivor.

"I definitely felt—you know, I left him, right?" Cole continues. "How are you supposed to justify that in the moment without having enough time to think about it?"

"So, you just decided you had to go, in order to live?"

"Yeah," Cole says softly. "Definitely a selfish act to a degree."

He also made up that he had seen Brett fall, further justifying his decision to leave him; and that Brett kept saying how much he loved his girls, something he thought would ease Brooke's pain when he had talked with her in Walton's running truck. He didn't tell his story for so long because he knew it had cracks in it, cracks that he had created. Brett was such a strong outdoorsman that Cole feared people wouldn't believe the truth—that Brett had made mistakes and then faded in the cold, leaving his novice partner no choice but to set off alone. And, in a way, he was right.

Immediately, Cole worries how he will be perceived when someone reads that he fabricated details. I tell him what his father has told him since that day: *Brett's death wasn't your fault.*

Cole has spent too long processing his guilt to be derailed by his admission. Even if Brett didn't say it, he knew the only way out was to keep going.

Perhaps that was the case with everyone. Perhaps it still is. As Joel says pointedly, "We see our own flaws in Brett."

We see our joys in him, too.

Cole biking on the Monarch Crest, 2024.

ACKNOWLEDGMENTS

Pls hold 2 pages

ACKNOWLEDGMENTS

274

CREDITS AND PERMISSIONS

Hold 1 page